gender +

CHRIST CENTERED SEXUALITY

Ennrich Kritzinger

malcolm down
PUBLISHING

WHAT OTHERS ARE SAYING...

I have known Ennrich for almost eight years. I'm delighted to say that we have become close friends. I see in Ennrich a man who cares very much for other people; that is the reason why he has written this book. I could go to him and share my deepest secrets and I'm confident he would have an understanding, caring and godly listening ear. The wisdom, incredible honesty, strength and hope relayed to you on the pages of this book have been hewn from his difficult life journey. I know you, the reader, will quite possibly reflect and change in subtle ways as you share in his story.

Everybody is thrilled when Ennrich comes to a gathering or party. Why? Because he is one of our favourite people; everyone he meets feels at home and safe with him. You will now encounter this incredibly honest man, a humble man, a man who has been broken by life but made new by a loving God. Enrich skilfully uses words to paint the picture of where he has been, where he is now and where he hopes and plans to go in the future. You will travel with him as he shares deeply and movingly; his honesty regarding the incredible change in his life will touch your soul.

This book is a love story, a love story made from heaven. My wife Trish and I watch Ennrich with his gorgeous wife Samantha as they move through life together and we marvel at the beautiful miracle God has wrought in and through them. Their love for each other is deep, real and heaven-sent. His story prompts me to exclaim: 'All things are possible with God!'

John Edwards
Author and founder of Walking Free Ministries

Ennrich is an incredible man who has experienced so much. I am proud to call him my friend. I am so pleased that he has finally written about his life and told the full, undiluted story.

I have been profoundly impacted and even brought to tears by this book. It's amazing to me how Ennrich somehow negotiated a pathway through such a challenging start in life. Many who experienced similar journeys didn't make it through this kind of thing, but it seems to me that God kept him as the apple of his eye for a divine purpose. I believe that purpose is to be a voice of truth and honesty for a generation that has lost its moral compass. To be a voice for those who are crying out for some kind of sense to the mess they are living in. To offer an empathetic road out for those who have been labelled and rejected as a misfit.

Ennrich's story will shock you but also warm your heart. It will enlighten you but also leave you asking questions. It will make you cry in one sentence, but then cause you to smile in the next. But most of all it will cause you to encounter the God who made a way for him where there seemed no way. That's the best part.

Mark Stevens

Worship pastor, songwriter and author

Ennrich has shared his story with honesty and integrity. He has led an interesting life and endured some very painful experiences. It would be understandable if he had given up. However, this book is testimony of his courage and the saving, healing power of Jesus Christ. It will surely be a source of great hope to others.

Paul Beadle

Joint national Leader, Living Waters UK

'Everything is beautiful in its time' says Ecclesiastes, and this book is a brilliant example of this principle.

I've known Ennrich for many years, and watched his passion

to help others grow and now find expression through the publication of his truly life-changing story. It is a book that offers hope for 'this time', a time when many are confused by same-sex attraction issues and the challenges of finding their God-created self.

It is a great read! But best of all, it inspires hope, offers the possibility of freedom and invites all to get involved in being part of the answer.

Stephen Matthew

Pastor, Resident Itinerant Ministry, Life Church, Bradford, UK

Ennrich's story is a must-read remarkable journey from beginning to end. It is a story of grace and redemption over guilt and rejection. He makes sense of what is one of the most confusing issues of our time in a brave, honest and straightforward way. I recommend it wholeheartedly.

Steve Gambill

Lead pastor, Life Church, Bradford, UK

ACKNOWLEDGEMENTS

My story in the form of this book could not have been possible without the support of family and friends, for which I am eternally grateful. Especially my wife and best friend, Samantha. Thank you, *'lief'* (beloved) for your unconditional love, understanding and support in our marriage; you are simply amazing. To my mother, Pierrette; thanks for your blessing and for releasing me to write this story. To my five proofreaders, dearest friend Taryn and my much-loved sister Anna; thank you for your time and dedication. The leadership and family of Life Church (lifechurchhome.com) in Bradford, Leeds, Belfast and Warsaw for your encouragement in standing with me. My editor, pastor Stephen Matthew (stephenmatthew.com), church builder and author that took my humble story and help make it this book. To good friends John Edwards (walkingfree.org) and Mark Stevens (markstevensmusic.com) for your prayers, positive confession and consistently speaking words of life over me. My publisher, Malcolm Down and Sarah Griggs for their wisdom and amazing contribution. Sem Schaap, my extremely creative Dutch friend responsible for the graphic design of the cover page and the genderplus.co.uk website. The greatest of thanks, glory and praise goes to my Father in heaven for his redeeming love, shown to me through his Son, my friend and Saviour Jesus. To his ever-faithful Spirit in guiding me through life and providing wisdom at every crossroad I have had to manoeuvre. I am eternally grateful for the privilege of being called into co-working for his kingdom.

CONTENTS

INTRODUCTION:
IT'S TIME
+ + +

'Everything is beautiful in its time' says the Bible, and I believe that now is the right time to share my story with whoever decides to pick this book up.

For many years I've wanted to tell it, not for its own sake or because it is a beautiful story in itself, but because it has been burning in my heart to be written. One of how sexual abuse can occur within any family, where relationships are complex and members relate to each other through their own brokenness. I've known for some years now that one day I should write it in away that would help others avoid some of my pain and, more importantly, enjoy some of my delights. And that takes time and patience. But we are here now. I do not write my story to point the finger, but to show how other people's actions have an effect in shaping our lives. Yet, by allowing God to have his way, he can re-shape us and make into the person he created us to be.

This story has now become my 'reason for being' and shapes my mission in life.

So here it is: Ennrich's story.

CHAPTER 1
ROOTS
+ + +

Like you, I am a product of my relational roots. Many relationships have shaped my life over the years, some good and others bad, but as with most people, family is where the shaping process began.

My parents both came from good, middle-class, South African farming backgrounds. On my dad's side, this consisted of a healthy helping of Protestant German-settler influence, combined with some Dutch ancestry. He grew up on a farm, but had forsaken the traditional responsibility of taking over after his father to provide ongoing support for the family. Instead, he moved to Cape Town in the late 1960s to work in the hide, leather and fur industry. This strained the family relationships, and the farm was taken over by his brother, my uncle, instead.

My ma, the eldest of four children, also came from a good, conservative family. Hers was a combination of French Huguenot and Dutch settler stock. She met my father at the same time as studying nursing at Grootte Schuur Hospital – that's the hospital where Professor Christiaan Barnard apparently conducted the world's first heart transplant surgery, if you will forgive my name-dropping so early on in the book!

Sadly, Ma lost her father when she was eighteen years old; though in many ways she lost him sooner because he had suffered a massive stroke when she was just thirteen, leaving him bedridden, without speech and partially paralysed. He had studied medicine, specialising in surgery; however, unlike my father, my granddad had 'done his duty' and went into farming full-time when his father passed away, to care for the land and provide for the family. As a result he was an angry unfulfilled medic, a man who suffered severe headaches due to an aneurysm in his brain, which eventually led to the stroke.

During his illness, he was completely dependent on my grandma who also had their four children under the age of thirteen to care for. But she did it. She took over the running of the farm and raised their four children. She was also a piano teacher and a very creative lady. But the thing that amazes me the most is that she was elected Farmer of the Year in South Africa, while Granddad was completely bedridden! She was one extraordinary woman. So, my ma was raised by an amazing lady.

When my parents met in that now-famous hospital, there was chemistry from the start, chemistry that resulted in my arrival. This was the late sixties and the 'Hippy Movement' was in full swing. Its anti-establishment emphasis on 'free love' must have seemed like utopia to them, given their conservative upbringing, and as their love awakened it soon became lust without caution, and I was conceived. To cut a potentially long story short, I was conceived rather early in their relationship.

Now what were they to do? Both families where heavily involved in the Dutch Reformed Church, well known for its high moral standards. What would the community think and say? So, to prevent huge embarrassment and shame on the family, they decided to marry as soon as possible. The rushed decision meant they were totally unprepared for the demands married life would place on them, never mind the demands of parenting me. So it was a rocky start but sadly, it was about to get worse.

My dad was an angry man with unresolved issues from his

past, and particularly with his parents. His own father had died when he was just a young man and he had no way of being able to resolve many of his emotional issues. The anger built up in him and began to be expressed in violence; initially emotional and verbal abuse, but occasionally he was physically violent too. And as in most violent relationships, his anger was mainly directed towards the ones he loved the most, in this case my ma.

She continued to put up with it until one day she discovered that he had been unfaithful to her and separated from him. At this point I was only a couple of months old, and Ma was expecting my younger brother, who is only ten and a half months younger than me. Separating from my dad must have been daunting, with two very small ones to care for. She must have been devastated.

They soon decided that the best thing to do for us all was to divorce. I had just turned one, and my brother was merely two months old when the divorce was finalised.

Ma was broken. She found herself carrying her young infant into church, with me not yet a toddler by her side, to have him baptised. She was alone and ashamed; a single parent. So, she moved back to my grandparents' farm to live with my grandmother.

She tried to make sense of her young life. But as I reflect back, I cannot get my head and heart around what it must have been like for her; the embarrassment, the shame, not to mention people's prejudice. People can be so cruel. I'm told that moving back to live with Grandma on the farm was not an easy thing to do, as she had warned my ma several times against her relationship with my dad. But there we were, living with my grandmother on her farm in the Western Cape. It was all hands on deck and no easy job with three generations in one house, so inevitably it did not last too long. We just had to move.

So when I was two, my Ma used her nursing qualifications and took a job as the superintendent of a residential nursing home for the elderly. The job came with accommodation, a flat that was spacious enough for the three of us. So we moved away from the farm, and Ma was able to start her life over again. I can remember those early years, even though I was so young. Ma was my whole world; Dad never came to visit us. To this day I don't know if he ever made an effort to even *try* to come and see my brother and me.

We had such fun at the nursing home. Looking back now, I realise that it must have been such a blessing to have two young children in the mix with so many grandparents around! I fondly remember running into the common room each day after breakfast. The sunlight streamed in through its large windows and I would spend my morning surrounded by the 'click clack' of knitting needles while someone read me a story or played a game with my brother and me. We especially loved the tea trolley – every nursing home has one – and we got what seemed like an endless stream of tasty treats from it. There is always time for tea in a home like the one I spent my years in as a toddler. Those were happy days. The old folk loved my younger brother and me; hugs and kisses were the order of the day, and we felt so spoiled.

Ma was very busy, of course, and I remember us having a Xhosa nanny called Grace, who took care of us while Ma was hard at work running the nursing home. Thinking back, I can't remember where she lived. But she was a black African girl in her early twenties and her job was to look after us. Boy, we loved her! We played leapfrog and hide-and-seek together in the beautiful grounds surrounding the home. Days seemed endless. Time was of no significance. Every day seemed to be one of sunshine when we spent it with Grace.

The only strange thing I recall about Grace is that she could never come to church with us. The nursing home was situated next to the church we attended, so every week Grace got us dressed in our Sunday outfits and then waved us off but never came. It seemed odd to me. But I well remember those outfits: they were from my mother's Aunt Kate. She was a formidable German lady who had fled Nazi Germany during the war and ended up in America, where she married my great-uncle and they subsequently moved to South Africa. She had brought us German *lederhosen* and woollen capes from one of her visits back to Bavaria. We looked so dapper, almost like twins, and got lots of attention at church. I loved the attention, but missed having Grace there, who had so faithfully dressed us. Why could she not come to church? I would ask. After all, she was my nanny! I now understand that apartheid robbed us of sharing that joy together, and that my child-like instincts were pure.

Snapshots of other memories filter into my mind as I recount these events, one being our first Christmas at the nursing home. It was wonderful. The nursing staff practised Christmas carols, *a cappella*-style, for days – simply bliss! Their singing was somehow comforting to me; beautiful and soothing. So much so that I didn't even notice I didn't have a dad at that time.

Those memories are so good. I had one big happy 'nursing-home family'. And it was enough for me.

CHAPTER 2
THE FARM
+ + +

When I was three, Ma met a farmer from the neighbouring district. They met at church where he was a deacon, and he was also on the church board. I can't remember much of their courtship, but he and Ma must have been a good match and he slowly wove himself into the tapestry of our family unit. I was too young to understand the 'love thing' between them, but the farmer was soon to become my stepfather.

He had lost his first wife in a tragic car accident and had been left with four young children. I really must to pause here because I have not really given much thought to what that must have been like for him – running a farm and caring for four children while dealing with the grief of losing his wife and their mother. I wonder how they came to terms with this trauma. Did they ever? Hindsight is a wonderful thing, and I am left wondering if our coming to the farm was just another complication for them to navigate alongside their raw grief.

Anyway, Ma and the farmer got married, after which we moved from the nursing home to his farm. It was quite a shock to my system; we became part of a family of eight overnight! But it didn't end there, because the farm was also home to at least twenty-five of his farmworkers and their children. So this was a radically new environment for me.

My stepfather was fifteen years older than Ma. His four

children were therefore much older than my brother and I. We were all strangers to each other. I just could not get myself to call him Dad. How could I call a stranger Dad? He still had to earn the privilege. We called him *'oom'* rather than 'father', which is Afrikaans for 'uncle'.

My first memories of the farm are mainly of fear and anxiety. To start with, I had never had a functioning father in my life, and now I had one. Then there was the sudden increase in family size. But most of all, the move from our life at the nursing home to the farm wrenched me from my many loving grandparents and nanny Grace in particular. I had entered a new and unfamiliar world that was very scary.

Back in the nursing home, my little brother and I often shared Ma's big double bed in our cozy flat, especially if we were upset about something. We would all snuggle in together; it was a place of security and warmth, a loving nest. But that went too. Now I found myself constantly on edge, trying to work out where I fitted into this big new world I had been dropped into. All the space was overwhelming, and all the people a big unknown.

On the day that we arrived at the farm, I remember hiding behind a massive dresser in the front room of the old Victorian farmhouse, together with my brother, trying to eat a bag of pick and mix sweets as quietly as possible, so that the others – my two stepbrothers and two stepsisters – would not hear us. We'd been given them as a 'sweetener' to make our transition more palatable. But I was simply not ready to share yet: not ready to share my sweets, my space, my brother, my bedroom or my ma.

It was hard work for us all to make this set-up work, but I gradually came to understand there were some good things about it. One I quickly appreciated was the space; a seemingly endless land that was now 'mine', unlike the old nursing home garden.

What a joy! It was absolutely beautiful; rich, fertile farmland, with a river of the clearest water you could ever imagine running right through it. It ran down from majestic mountains and watered the fields surrounding our new home.

We were fortunate in South Africa; we started school at the age of six. So I had three glorious years to explore this endless tract of farmland, as well as the great new adventure of learning what farming was all about.

But family life remained a big challenge for me. The old Victorian farmhouse proved to be too small for us all. It was bursting at the seams. Sleeping arrangements were tricky, as there were now six children to find beds for. So in those early years we had to share rooms and sometimes beds to make it all work.

We ended up sharing beds, boys in one and girls in another. The sharing part was not unfamiliar as my brother and I had shared my mother's bed. But this was different. My two stepbrothers' presence was very different to my ma's.

I've often reflected back on that formative season in my life. At the time I assumed that sharing a bed with a much older boy/man was 'normal'. But was it? Did it set me up for what was to come? Or was it the yearning for a father figure that made me vulnerable; that made me trust so easily? I still sometimes wonder.

My stepfather and I could not get on. I didn't know how to trust him, nor did he give me a reason to do so. So I started to find security at night in my older stepbrother because he was kind to me. His presence in the bed began to feel strangely comforting; it was familiar enough to remind me of the many times I had snuggled up with Ma and my brother, yet very different too. By now I was four years old and this was the first time that any man had been so close to me. Sometimes in my sleep he would embrace me. Why was this all so comforting, so right? It seemed to fill a void that I did not even know was there; a void I did not know needed filling or knew how to fill.

The months passed. They became years. I still could not get on with my stepfather, and my stepbrother became the only man I trusted, respected and allowed to come close to me. He was more than ten years my senior. I looked up to him; he had become the one who filled the void my father had left, emotionally and physically. But this was soon to come to an end.

As my stepbrothers proceeded into puberty, we were split up into different rooms. In the new arrangement my little brother and I shared a room adjoining our parents, and it was then that things really started to kick off with my stepfather.

I became scared at night without my stepbrother. I missed him and the closeness we had. It was a strange room with new shadows on the walls that were enhanced and distorted by the bright moonlight. Barn owls on the roof added their haunting calls to the sounds made by the wind that frequently howled around the corners of the old farmhouse. I would gently rock myself to sleep. I didn't tell anyone I was afraid, I just kept on rocking; trying to reassure myself, comfort myself. I would lift my leg while lying on my stomach and then let it drop back, ever so gently down onto the mattress. Each thump was calming, rhythmically easing the anxiety I felt in my little beating heart, slowing it down with each thump on that mattress. Finally, I would drop off to sleep, but somehow, my subconscious mind continued the rocking and leg thumping on the mattress.

Then I would be woken up, startled by the first blow, by my stepfather beating me! I had woken him with the thumping of my leg. I had meant for it to comfort me, not wake the house. He never spoke to me, he just thrust a couple or so blows into my body under the sheets. It didn't seem to matter what his fist fell on.

This would silence me for the night, nothing more. Why did he never sit with me or comfort me or ask why – why I was scared?

I couldn't look him in the eyes in the morning; he and I never really spoke. Fortunately breakfast was rushed enough, getting six children through it before school started for the older children. So I never had the time, the need or desire to talk to him. I was scared of him. I hated him.

He was a very strict man. He had now become an elder in our local church and started each day with a Bible reading and prayers after breakfast. I fell asleep on the kitchen bench too many times to count, warmed by the Aga stove on a winter's morning. But then I would be jolted awake, as it was the custom for us all to kneel down when we prayed. I regarded my stepfather as an authoritarian figure who ruled from a distance – untouchable and unapproachable. When we ever did have words, it was usually him telling me off while giving me a good hiding, which of course I deserved. Or did I?

Reflecting back, I now realise that my brother and I were just a hindrance to him. He needed a new wife to help raise his children, and my little brother and I were additional mouths to feed. Did his attitude towards me contribute towards driving me to look for love elsewhere, or was it my choice? Did I detach from him in defence, or in fear of getting hurt? But then, how do you speak to someone that just beats you up and never takes the time to speak or hear you out?

I missed my stepbrother so much during the day and couldn't wait for him to get back from school to spend some time with him. He wasn't always kind; he would mock me and call me names. Sometimes he would look at me as if to say, 'What do you want?' I developed an anxious facial tick, a twitch that just increased the mocking. I loved and hated him all at the same time; he had no clue how to handle the affection I craved and wanted from him. Yet there was this strong connection between us. Or was it just me, something I had imagined?

By the time I was six, my older stepbrothers were well into adolescence. I can't specifically remember any sexual touch during those first years on the farm. I'm not sure if this was my mind's way of blocking out what had actually happened, or if it was all muddled up in the desire to know love and affection from him, a sort of father figure. All I can remember is him; his warm comforting weight, his smell that was different, not like Ma's.

And how it happened, how it all started, still remains a mystery to me. He embraced me as usual, but then started to touch me; he touched me in *that* way. One vivid memory I have is finding myself in his bedroom one day, hiding under the bed, naked, with his body pressed against me. Why were we under the bed, naked, hiding? Why did it all feel so wrong, dirty, and why did I feel such guilt, such shame? Yet I trusted him and yes, I loved him. Well, at least I thought I did. What did I truly know of love at that age?

Nobody knew about it, about us.

He was a handsome man, very bright and extremely good at sport, especially athletics. He was head boy of his class and school. Was all this performance to get accepted, appreciated and loved? Was he not also just looking for love, acceptance, someone to hold or to be held? Was it out of anger and frustration, trying to manage his own puberty? Or was physical touch just his way of interpreting love? So many 'why's' behind what happened. Why, then, this thing between us?

I, on the other hand, was just a child; a creative, sensitive child. He should have known better, he should have known not to do the things we did, the things nobody knew about. Yet why was I left feeling so guilty?

CHAPTER 3
GROWING PAINS
+ + +

My ma plunged herself into life on the farm. She loved the land and would have made an amazing farmer herself.

Her ancestral farm came to the family in the late 1600s when the Cape of Good Hope was still under the rule of the Dutch East India Company. Ma's earliest ancestor was a Frenchman who came to work as the first veterinary surgeon, looking after the animals, especially the horses kept at the Dutch *kasteel* (castle) in Cape Town. The story goes that when the Dutch East India Company became bankrupt, they gave her early ancestors a huge amount of land to the west of the country, reaching all the way to the coast, and the farm remained in the family for many generations. It had its own veterinary practice, wine cellars, a flour mill, various workshops including a forge, and several cottages occupied by staff to run the big house.

Ma was the eldest of the four children born to my *'oupa',* which means grandpa. He had desperately wanted a son as his firstborn, but got Ma. In fact, he was so ready to name his firstborn son that when my ma was born he gave her a name that is the diminutive of the family name, so convinced was he that she would be a boy. So when the time came for the land to be passed on, it went to his third-born, the only son, much to my ma's disappointment.

Nevertheless, here she was, finally on a farm, a place that reminded her so much of her childhood. Dreams awakened that she had long ago laid to rest. She was in her element, and flourished.

Ma had the mammoth task of raising and feeding us, while simultaneously running a small dairy business from the farm which provided more than twenty families with creamy milk from our Jersey cows. Alongside this she would prepare rations for all the farmworkers and their families and, of course, be doing school runs and the never-ending task of laundry. She was mother, nurse, businesswoman and farmer. How she did it all I will never know, but I have the utmost respect for her.

The National Party had governance at the time, and apartheid was the system. Working conditions, health and education for the farmworkers was atrocious – not that it had been any better before apartheid – but something had to be done. So Ma started with getting a small church service going in one of the coach houses on a Sunday. The minister at the local missions outreach was a good friend, and so he would come and help out.

Christmas was another opportunity to do something special, and we always gave the workers well beyond the rations and wages due for working on the farm. Ma was good that way, looking after not only the workers but their families as well. I can still vividly remember all those farmworkers' children dressed in their new outfits on Christmas morning; so beautiful with their big smiling faces. They had become my new friends, although I was never supposed to mention that.

Yes, the farm was an oasis of treasures and delicious crops – mostly citrus fruit, wheat, vegetables, figs and watermelon. There was always so much to do. We created gangs, teaming up with the farmworkers' children to play 'cowboys and crooks' against each other. There never seemed to be enough hours to fill the days with all the fun that was to be had.

Ma's nursing background and caring personality were always sought out when help was needed. I remember it being particularly drawn on during the tuberculosis outbreak of the 1970s, which reached epidemic proportions. It was very severe amongst farmworkers in the Western Cape. Remember, at that time South Africa was a country already oppressed by poor leadership during the apartheid regime, and further burdened by sanctions against it from the rest of the world. It was a task that called for a small army as Ma poured her life into helping others while still running ours with a sickly workforce. But she did it.

She was a star, but my dear ma knew very little about my deep needs. How could she know? I never shared them. And I always felt like everyone and everything else mattered more than us, more than me. She gradually became another distant parent, out of reach and far too busy for me.

The summer before I was to start school, my sister was born. Now we were seven children and two adults. I can't even remember Ma being pregnant. It was never announced or shared with the family that she was expecting; just all of a sudden there was another child in the home. My brother and I were so jealous of our new sister. It seemed that what little attention and love there was for us children was now focused on her, and I was shipped off to the big new world of school.

School was a whole new experience for this 'farm boy'. I was a creative child, placed in a top-heavy academic and sports school, where art and creativity were neither celebrated nor encouraged. Maybe it's not surprising, then, that schooling became secondary in importance to me. My head was filled with all but getting an education. I wanted to create, not be contained. I had no attention span. I could not concentrate and did not want to be there.

I remember being completely engrossed in drawing pictures

of mermaids and fantastic sea creatures, a form of escapism from this new reality in which I found myself. I was forever in trouble with the teachers for not listening. I remember being made to wear an Alice band with donkey ears on it, and when I spoke out of turn had red masking tape stuck across my mouth – which left awful stains once removed that could not be concealed. The other kids mocked, teased and bullied me too. I hated them. They did not understand me, nor did I trust them; I did not know how to trust. I did not understand why I was being punished for being myself, for being creative. I soon concluded, 'This small-town school has no room for me.'

School soon became an existence to be tolerated. I hated it but, of course, I still had to go, even if they misunderstood and bullied me for not respecting my teacher's authority. I simply did not know how to, nor did I want to. All I knew of authority was a distant, authoritarian stepfather who beat me. I was too scared to trust my teachers – in fact, any adults in positions of authority. I was frightened to have them close to me. I mean, what would happen if I did? Could I even risk it? So I looked at grown-ups with a question mark on my face... Can I trust you? Can you be trusted?

Just before I turned eight, in my second year of school, Ma called my brother and I into the kitchen one afternoon. She was sat at the kitchen table, her eyes all puffy from crying. As she held my shoulders, she broke the news to us that our father had died in a car accident. I was initially stunned, and recall my brother simply saying, 'Peter's dad died too' as he ran off to play outside. Peter was one of his school friends who recently lost his father. It was all my brother's young mind could grasp of the situation.

It was then that I fully realised for the first time in my life that I had always had a real dad. He had always been out there somewhere. At any time he could have come and rescued me from all of this, but now that was impossible because he was dead. My whole world fell apart right there in the kitchen. I remember running to my bedroom and closing the door. I cried myself to sleep that night, and for many nights in the months that followed. In the same moment that I had discovered I had a real father, he had been removed forever. Death is so final. We sang 'What a friend we have in Jesus' at his funeral. If only I had known that then!

The three of us found ourselves standing at an open grave, scattering rose petals onto the closed casket of a stranger. Refreshments followed at an aunt's house, my dad's sister, someone else I had never met before. We were surrounded by a family we had never known; just more strangers. It was all too weird. Surreal. And to make things worse, I wanted to see my dad's body; I wanted to say hello and goodbye, properly. But Ma said 'no' because he had suffered severe head injuries and she did not want me traumatised. 'What do you mean, traumatised?' I asked. It was a bit too late to start worrying about me being traumatised!

My world had been tossed upside down. All I can remember are the emotions of severe sorrow: hurt, fear, anger, grief, pain, loneliness and shock, all at the same time. I had not been prepared for this. I had no idea how to deal with my loss, or with everything else that had happened to me since we moved to the farm.

More and more dissociation from reality followed. All I did was cry for something like six months after my father's death. My mother was out of her depth with me. We ended up on the doorstep of a child psychologist, and after some counselling and tests, I was diagnosed with attention deficit hyperactivity disorder (ADHD) – a hyperactive child – and was started on

Ritalin immediately. It was the fashionable cure in the 1970s.

At school, my relationships suffered even more. At assembly on the Monday morning after the funeral, the headmaster, who did not even know I existed, made an announcement that the two Kritzinger boys had lost their father. My world came crashing down. Not only was I in the middle of all of this emotional turmoil, but now everybody else knew about it. I felt so exposed. Grown-ups and children can be so cruel. And so the bullying continued.

One older boy in particular seemed to live off the thrill of calling me all sorts of names. He would seek me out, and no matter how hard I tried to keep to myself, and hide from him, he would find me, mock me and humiliate me. 'Hey, sissy!' he would call. 'Still drawing all your pretty pictures? You're a faggot, you are queer!'

I became used to his constant name-calling and would try my best to let the words run off me and not affect me. But every word stung and hooked into the core of my heart, adding to the turmoil that was already going on within my young self. They just affirmed the shame I already felt.

However, today was different; I don't know why but I just couldn't take it anymore. I could not just stand there. I could not feel this hurt, this pain and shame any longer. Something snapped in me that day, and all I could feel was anger. The room turned red. All I could see was that bully's face and the jar of porcupine quills – probably meant for educational decoration. The next thing I remember was stabbing him with a porcupine quill, pushing it as deep into his arm as my seven-and-a-bit-year-old strength would allow. The rush of emotions hit: absolute satisfaction followed by overwhelming shock and guilt as it dawned on me what I had just done. Without a thought or comment, I grabbed my book bag and ran out of the classroom and walked all the way home to the farm.

Nobody ever questioned this. I mean, I stabbed a boy! Not my parents, not the teacher, nor his parents, or the principal of the school. How strange was this? Or did they know he was a bully? His dad was the local doctor, our family doctor, and my ma knew him very well. How could this be? Health and safety would have been all over it today, not to mention the authorities. Why did we never speak about this? Why did we never get to the root of it all? Too many 'whys'!

I drifted deeper and deeper into my own world where my relationship with boys were strangely detached and yet I cautiously pursued them for friendship. I was one of them but just could not relate to them at all. Hanging out mostly with the girls did not help my situation, but at least I was not alone.

My schoolwork was average, but I did, however, excel in extra art classes and languages. Sadly, art was not a subject at this school. I began to get on well with some of the teachers, especially the female staff. The men just scared me. I craved acknowledgement from them, and would have done just about anything to get some. I did not know how to handle them nor how to respond around them, yet I was supposed to be one of them; I just felt awkward, distant and insecure.

Throughout this period, the sexual abuse from my stepbrother continued, as did the beatings from the 'oom'. I was not finding my place in this new family, I'd lost the father I never had, was constantly bullied at school and the distancing of Ma and everything else all drove me closer to my abusive stepbrother. He was the only solace I had, so my hurt and desperate need for comfort drove me more and more into his confidence. I was looking for something; I just did not know what.

Was I just trying to fill the void of not knowing the love of my father, a father I didn't even know but was now gone? Was I trying to replace the emptiness with sexual encounters? Did I even understand I was doing that? The sad truth is that I did not know any better, and it would have been ludicrous to even think about questioning what was happening at the time. I didn't even know that it was all so wrong.

CHAPTER 4
FILLING THE VOID
+ + +

And then he was gone. At eighteen my stepbrother left home to do his national service and he left my life. I longed for him. The abuse stopped, but the damage was done.

Still only a child, all I felt was a void inside me, a void that kept growing. I had no dad, a distant ma, a stepfather I hated, and the only form of love I had from a man – well, what I thought was love – had now gone too.

I was dying on the inside for love, for touch, for him, for something. My sexual awareness was heightened. I would pleasure myself, trying to feel some sense of comfort, of release, to the point of it hurting. At least the pain made me feel something.

But life has to go on. So I kept on doing life with everyone on the farm. It was then that I started noticing the other men – the farmworkers and their sons. I was about to fall into an early puberty, like a badly bruised fruit that ripened too early, and I had no idea what to do with it. Where and what was to be my example of becoming a man?

I was jealous of the relationships many of the farmworkers had with their sons. I wanted it; I wanted it so badly. I craved it and I hated the farmworkers for having it. I despised myself for not having it. Why? Why did Dad have to die and leave me like this? Some relief came in the shape of my parents deciding to have the old Victorian farmhouse refitted. The old chicken coop, now overgrown with rambling roses, got a brand-new roof so it could become our makeshift kitchen. A gas cooker was fitted, and the room was powered up for a fridge-freezer. I enjoyed this creative adventure, because it took my mind off the rest of my inner angst. It was awesome having meals outside in the temporary 'coop-chen', overlooking the building work.

And the farm still had to be run. My brother and I took it in turns to ride the tractors with the farmworkers, riding along as they ploughed and harvested the fields. It was a fun opportunity to sit on their laps and hold the steering wheel, pretending to drive.

It was on one such occasion that I noticed the closeness of a particular 'brown boy' that got to share the steering wheel with me. He was more or less my age and we really got on. We became good friends, but it got to a point where we started experimenting with touching each other and kissing. I was infatuated. He was different. Nobody could know of this. We had to hide our friendship; not only was he a boy, but a boy of colour. It was heading for the 1980s and the height of apartheid, so we would have been severely punished for it. He might have even been killed, and I would have been sworn to silence for ever. It was all too much of a risk, too much to lose. To say the least, it ended rather abruptly. To me it was more loss. If we had ever been caught, what shame and embarrassment it would have been for our 'white' family: me and the 'boy', the 'brown' boy.

As I headed into puberty, I experienced ever-increasing difficulties relating to my own gender and peers. The bullying and name-calling continued to the point where my own siblings began to join in and joke about me. It's strange how those words and names had the power to shape my thinking about myself, my self-image. Maybe they were right. How and why did I believe them? I felt unable to relate to being a boy or a man, and I even wished I wasn't one. At least if I was a girl I would have been liked and loved more. I despised my own body. I despised my own gender.

Eventually my youngest stepsister left the farm to do her final year of school. She was the youngest of the stepchildren. Things were not good at home. Constant arguing between our parents made her decide to move into the boarding school that was attached to the school we all went to. I was now the oldest male left in the house. I felt an increasing pressure to perform, but never felt adequate enough to deliver according to the demands of living and working on the farm. My older stepbrothers had been so much better at the whole farming business than me, and that did not help my feelings of inadequacy. The frustration was tangible sometimes. Being able to help meant that I felt included, accepted.

I suffered with various allergies, including wheat dust, which would set off my wheeziness. Of course, during harvest-time it was at its worst, so I was never asked to help with the harvest – too much risk, I suppose. But I perceived this as yet more rejection.

Life continued on the farm. Fields had to be ploughed for wheat and winter crops; the 300-plus Merino sheep had to be shorn after the winter and before the lambing. All this was done manually by a group of black farmworkers from the Transkei, a homeland created for mostly Xhosa-speaking black South Africans. They came each year to sheer the sheep. They could not stay on the farm because they were black and the farmworkers, brown; they did not mix, nobody mixed. How crazy!

The freshly shorn fleece would be graded and thrown into extra-large bags hung from wooden frames. My little brother and I had to trample the wool down and compress it into these bags, getting as much weight into each bag as possible because the bale of wool was sold by weight. This was so much fun. We got to hang out with all the men; each time a fleece was thrown over the side of the bag, the volume in the bag grew. This meant we were one step closer to seeing over the wooden frame to what was happening on the barn floor. By the end of the day we were covered with lanolin and had the softest skin after a hot bath that night. What a juxtaposition – soft skin, great memories amongst all the dysfunction… my emotions were all over the place.

Then in the midst of this full life on the farm, my parents decided to enlarge it by buying the neighbouring farmer's land which had come up for sale. He was a single man who looked after his widowed ma. I can't remember much about him other than that he would drop in now and again, was softly spoken and rather unkempt in his appearance, with a big beard. Sometimes he smelt of booze.

The land he owned was beautiful. It stretched all the way into the Cederberg mountains. The land was as unkempt as he was, but this added to its charm; an untamed wilderness ready for me to explore. I couldn't wait!

Back at home, the pressure of the new venture caused tensions to mount. Ma and my stepfather fought constantly about money, running the farms, the children and so on. The house was big and they tried to keep their screaming matches as far away from us as possible, but we all knew about them. Violence was also in amongst it all, never in front of us, but ever-present.

Around that time, one Saturday my younger brother had the opportunity to go and shoot some game. The rule was that no rifle was to be left unattended at any time. If a rifle was your responsibility, it was your responsibility at all times. Well, my brother forgot his rifle and left it leaning against one of the farmworker's cottages when he went for a drink of water or something. When my parents found out, all hell broke loose. Ma caned him so hard and so long, he begged and begged and screamed and screamed. I was in the bedroom next to his, sobbing my heart out. I thought she was going to kill him.

I felt so helpless and pathetic. All those years of my ma being hurt and abused, all those years of violence and fighting had finally found an opportunity to be vented. She seemed to be releasing so much contained emotion and my poor little brother was on the receiving end of it. I hated her for it; I hated myself for not being able to step in and rescue him or do something about it. I resented her for hitting him so hard. I was a mess.

Meanwhile, our social life as a family carried on as normal, the tensions and personal pain all well hidden beneath a cloak of respectability. My parents were actively involved in the local community. There was the farmer's union, the school board and the church board, not to mention a variety of sports clubs. The refurbished farmhouse became a hub of entertainment as all our curious friends, neighbours and goodness knows who else would turn up to have a tour of it. It became the home of the local ladies' group from church and, because a piece of our land was used by the school as a training circuit for rugby and triathlon, a steady stream of sports teams and coaches came through too.

Even though my stepbrothers had now left to do their national service and later university, they were gifted, and had drawn a crowd of people into our world. These friends were always received with open arms, as entertaining was a big part of our culture. And for the most part, having the house full of interesting people was fun and created good memories for me. The downside was that it gave me a lot to compete with. My parents' time and ability to give their love and attention was already spread sparsely without all this entertaining. But that's the way it was.

In the midst of buying the new farm, Grandma (*Ouma*) came to help carry some of the weight of all the changes that went alongside it. That was a great blessing to the children, for we loved her and she was good to all of us.

One afternoon during her stay, Ma decided to take us to the new farm in the *'bakkie'* – which is South African slang for a pick-up truck. Grandma joined her in the front and we three youngest children were on the back. We stood on the back of the *bakkie*, holding onto the bull bar, loving the fresh air beating on our faces as she drove along at full speed. I discovered that if you hold your head at just the right angle, with an open mouth in the wind, you could produce some 'wind songs'! Life was good, sometimes. And this was one of them. On we drove in the warm afternoon breeze, through citrus orchards and natural veld, spotting the baboons that frequented the roadside as they searched for any oranges that may have fallen off passing wagons. On arriving at the new farm we drove straight past the homestead to one of the older orchards. And there we saw them. We were still stood on the back so couldn't miss it. To our horror we had just stumbled across our stepfather and a much younger woman in a very compromising situation in her car. I remembered her and this car, it was a brown Peugeot.

It transpired that he had met this young woman, a teacher, at one of the social events up at our refurbished farm and, unbeknown to us all, he had pursued her. Ma and the rest of us had absolutely no idea, but it was now all out in the open, quite literally.

I could see Ma was devastated through the back window of the pick-up, as she reasoned with *Ouma*. For the second time in her life she was losing a husband due to unfaithfulness. My heart ached and sank. A strange silence fell on the back of the *bakkie* as we just looked at each other. My poor little sister saw it too; this was her dad and the teacher in the car. It was dreadful.

We were all sitting down on the trip back to our farm. Silence and despair filled the space between us on the back of the *bakkie*. I was twelve and a half, my brother eleven and my little sister barely six, but we knew what we had just seen was not good. Ma tried to hide it, but the silent conversation between her and *Ouma* spoke volumes.

She was now driving faster than usual. I could almost feel her need to understand, to get to the bottom of this. On arriving on the farm she dropped the three of us with *Ouma* and she set off again. *Ouma* said she was going to see the local reverend of our church. We kids were to play outside as if nothing had happened. But something did just happen. It was chaos, the silent type.

I was so angry and disappointed. I felt rejected yet again by another father. I hated him for it. And the endless stream of questions flooded my mind once more: Did the schoolteacher seduce him, or did he choose to leave us? Were we not worth staying for? Was I not worth sticking around for? And who else knew about this? I discovered the teacher resided at a boarding school where my youngest stepsister was now staying. Surely she must have known something about her father and this teacher? Surely others must have known? But did they? I tried to make sense of it all. We all felt so cheated, so betrayed.

Ma and Stepdad got home late that evening. We were all in bed when they returned but I could hear them quarrelling. *Ouma* came to my room to comfort me; we made small talk to hide what was happening in the farmhouse kitchen. Just what was happening there or what was said I still do not know. But the atmosphere in the house after that day was cold as ice; all eye contact ceased. The 'elephant in the room' was so big that it pressed everyone against the walls and nobody dared to address it. I desperately wanted to talk, to talk to someone, to try to understand. But I couldn't. I just wanted to cry.

Back at school after this dreadful weekend I had to sit a test, which I failed miserably. The problem was that I could not study for it because I could not concentrate at home. So the teacher took me and some other boys who had failed to the boy's cloakroom and gave us a hiding for failing. Corporal punishment was still the order of the day. After my three strikes with the cane, he asked me, nonchalantly, why I had not done the preparation for this test. In that moment I gathered the courage and told him that things were falling apart at home.

He knew my parents very well because he was the PE teacher and his various sports teams used our land regularly for training. Furthermore, the teacher that was caught with my stepdad was his colleague. I didn't know whether he knew it was her, he just looked at me with a blank face when I told him. And that was it, end of conversation.

'Doesn't anyone care about this, or us, or me?' I wanted to yell. 'Thanks, sir, thanks for nothing!' I hated him for not caring enough to do something. He was just another adult, just another disappointment.

What followed was an absolutely crazy two weeks. My stepbrothers came home from university and wanted to know what had happened. Nobody spoke directly with each other and I didn't know what to tell them; I did not fully understand it myself. Anyway, why must I be the one to answer their questions?

'I just saw them in the car, in the orchard,' I said. 'You go and ask them!'

Then the packing began. Everything belonging to my brother, sister and I was packed into the big Mercedes truck. We would be going to live with Grandma. It is all a blur as I reflect back on it. But I do remember that in those two weeks prior to our departure, my younger brother and I lashed out in anger towards my stepfather. One evening my brother burst into the bathroom, where my parents were quarrelling, with a loaded hunting rifle, and threatened to end it all, end him, our stepdad. All civilised ways of expressing emotion had ceased to exist. It was typically immature behaviour at the time, but at least it was a way to release the anger and hurt he felt. How do you express the frustration and disappointment he felt at the tender age of eleven?

Towards the end of the week, my little brother sneaked up to our stepdad's office where all the wages were kept for paying the farmworkers. He took handfuls of banknotes and brought them down to me. I was a little surprised and scared that we might get caught, yet I knew in my heart that this was the last time we would get any money from him. The day before we got into that Mercedes truck and drove away from the farm, my brother and I broke every tractor, truck and harvester, every farm vehicle we could find. We were hurting, and it was our way of hurting him for hurting us.

Worst of all was that our stepfather continued with the affair. Was it not worth giving up for us? Was it not worth giving it up for me? Perhaps it was because he knew that he would have no obligation to look after my brother and I once the divorce was through. We had no rights to his money, his farm or any land, because we were never really his. He wasn't our dad after all; our dad was dead.

Ever wondered what being 'thrown away' feels like? Like a piece of dirt or rubbish? That day was the closest I have ever been to that feeling. I can't even remember if I said goodbye to anyone; we just left. We left that farm as if all that we had known and done there for the last ten years just didn't matter at all.

I never saw my stepbrothers, stepsisters or stepfather again. The loss was heartbreaking and so unnecessary.

I can't find words to describe what Ma must have felt. The shock, the betrayal, the pain and embarrassment were devastating. Here she was, divorcing for the second time and running from it all again. Keeping busy and running hard may distract us from the immediate pain of events like this, but it doesn't take the pain away. Where we go, the pain goes.

Living with Grandma was only a temporary measure. But it gave Ma the space and time she needed to come to terms with the new situation. She desperately wanted to make things normal and stable for us. But could she ever? She certainly tried, and was soon out looking for work to ensure we were fed and clothed. It was back to basics for us as a family.

Another immediate implication of all this was that we had to move schools in the middle of the academic year. Not ideal, and as a result we ended up in three different schools in two different towns.

We never spoke about the emotional turmoil that persisted in our personal worlds; there was too little room for it. And Ma was hurting so much that my brother and I kept it mostly to ourselves. When it did come out it was in rage, lashing out at each other. We just had no way of dealing with the trauma.

I blamed some of it on my little sister – at least she still had a dad, a link back to all the people I felt I had lost. How unfair that was of me. But she saw her dad every second weekend and we never saw him. On one occasion he came to pick her up in his brand-new German sedan. There it was, proudly parked outside our humble little rented house; I despised him for having a new car, with his new wife, on their new farm. I felt so cheated. Was there ever going to be room for us, anywhere? Would there ever be room for me? I took a red permanent marker pen and scribbled, 'I hate you' all over his new car. I needed to hurt him once more. Hurt him back.

We tried going to church, but Ma just cried. She cried for all she had lost, for all the pain and hurt, and the unspoken silent label she now wore of being a twice-divorced woman. The new congregation didn't know us or anything about us, but how do you even begin to share what had happened? It was embarrassing and we did not feel welcome. We never went back to church as a family.

I was numbed by it all. Not only had I lost my room, my space, the farm, school, friends, brothers, sisters, and a stepfather, but I had also lost my ma. I had lost the ability to speak to her, the boldness to speak up. So I shut down. I was desperate to talk about all that had happened, but Ma was hurting so much, I didn't know how to go there. I was scared of exploding and blaming her for leaving the farm. I couldn't trust my own emotions, for there were so many of them. I was angry at Ma for responding the way she had. What I mean is, that she could have stayed on at the farm and worked it out. I was angry at myself for not confronting her about it, and angry at Ma for creating a situation where not one of us was able to speak for all the emotion we had bottled up inside. I secretly blamed her for it all; for being an emotional wreck and for leaving no safe space to speak about our now messed-up lives.

We had been living with *Ouma* for six months when Ma was offered a full-time job working at a local primary health care clinic in the Western Cape in a small town called Hopefield. Even the name of this little town should have been a clue, bringing us some relief! But it all felt so hopeless. The job took her away during the week. So we stayed with *Ouma*. My little sister and I attended the same small school in the village, which catered for all ages, while my brother went off to boarding school. My ma split us two boys up because we were angry and a handful after the divorce. My brother was near to where my uncle and aunt lived. They were quite close and my uncle took him under his wing in a way, which became another relationship that I didn't have. I was jealous of him and what they had together at this time.

I did speak to *Ouma* about some of the stuff in my heart. But mostly I cried. At least when I cried, I could get rid of some of the emotion, but only some. She listened and just let me be. Many late nights followed with long chats and many tears. She couldn't answer my 'whys?' because they were questions for Ma, and I couldn't go there. Have you ever experienced a situation where someone is hurting so much that they just freeze up? Well, I felt like that, completely frozen. So I hid deeper inside myself.

One afternoon Ma and I did have words. And it almost came out. But instead I walked out of the kitchen and slammed the door. She called me back and made me open and close the door 100 times properly, without slamming it, counting every time.

A friend of *Ouma's* arrived while this was going on which increased my embarrassment, but I had to keep going with the door. The hate built within me with every count of that door. I hated Ma for leaving, for us being alone again, for money being tight and for punishing me in this childish way. It was so degrading and embarrassing. How dare she… She was the adult and had made life-altering decisions that affected me, and now here she was dictating how I should respond in my anger. I got to 97-98-99, then walked outside and with all my strength slammed the door behind me on the count of 100. I left, and in my mind I had left her, left them, it was over with us. I was done with her. She lost me and I lost her. It was better that way, safer, I thought.

In the weeks that followed I was invited to go and visit my uncle and aunt on my mother's family farm. It was weird! I found myself walking around the farm seeing how much everyone else had, and I had nothing. Nothing was left of a possible inheritance I could have shared in because of the choices made by those who were supposed to be my dad, my parents. It fuelled my hate once more.

I hated this family – my family – for having wealth, and despised myself because of our lack. In reaction to it all I took a small gold chain from my aunt's dressing room table. My *nefie* (cousin) saw me, but I didn't care, I just took it. I wanted something as well, something that was mine. Later *Ouma* confronted me about it. I lied and told her I picked it up on the beach – 'It must have washed ashore!' I proclaimed. But she knew the truth, took it from me, and, in her gentle way, gave it back to them.

I didn't know if Ma knew about any of this. But if she did, why did she not confront me? Or did she know but was scared of what I might have had to say? I blamed her for leaving my dad and my stepfather. Her reaction to past events had also caused us our present dilemma. I wanted to provoke her but she didn't rise to it. She left it to *Ouma* to deal with and just ran from it.

My anger was unappeased yet again.

CHAPTER 6
BOARDING SCHOOL
+ + +

It was tough on Ma, but overall more beneficial financially to have both of us boys in boarding school while she worked full-time to support us. My stepfather had no financial obligation towards my brother and me, so Ma had to make ends meet. That meant we had to stay in boarding school most weekends, and ended up seeing her maybe one weekend in a month. I hated it. I missed a home life so much.

Meanwhile, my little sister – who was also sent away to a new boarding school – would see her dad, my stepfather, every second weekend, as had been decided by the courts. I was so jealous of her being able to go back and see the farm and what was once familiar; a safe place, as I fundamentally remembered it now. By this time our stepfather had married the teacher and she was now pregnant with their first child. She was more than thirty years younger than him, which could not have been easy for my sister to get her head around.

Boarding school was a whole new concept to me. It consisted mainly of boys from the inner-city schools in and around Cape Town, many of who were troubled youngsters. They had been shipped out to the rural schools to be sorted out, but it felt more like 'out of sight, out of mind'. They joined boys like my brother and I from single-parent families, and an assortment of local farm boys whose homes were so far away that commuting to school was impossible.

At first, boarding school was a big shock. Sometimes fun, sometimes funny, but mostly like boot camp. It was new and tough. I was in the first year of high school – and had to endure a year of initiation where we as the juniors were expected to do all sorts of favours for the seniors; things like polishing their shoes, making their beds and carrying their schoolbags. We ended up doing all sorts of crazy favours for them; it was the custom, and we did not know any better.

We sat in ranking order at the table in the dining room. The seniors got their food first and we had to obey their every command. It was kept playful for the most part, but you knew that if you didn't do what was expected, the other juniors would suffer for it. It was the fear of making it tough for others that kept everyone in their place.

I had to share a room with five other boys, which I hated. And to complicate matters further, one of the live-in teachers was a cousin of my aunt. He had been asked to keep an eye on me, a role he took seriously by making it his personal mission to come and show me how to make my own bed! Ridiculous. I just wanted to be left alone and forget the last few years. I wanted to make a clean start, create a new name for myself and be a new person. I wanted to be incognito and he was in danger of blowing my cover!

Boarding school was also a place where great friendships were formed, mainly because we were all in the same boat. Some relationships were healthy, others not so. I recall some of the prefects did a great job in caring for those more junior than themselves. Then, on the other hand, there were quite a few cliques centred on historic bad behaviours like gang membership, smoking or taking drugs. Some boys had been abusing alcohol for years.

It was there that I did my first haircut. How difficult could it be? I thought. Some of the junior boys needed haircuts, which they would normally get at home on weekends. But we couldn't all go home on weekends, and some of the kids came from poor families and couldn't really afford a haircut. So I gave it a try. I was the only one gutsy enough to do it! Well, it soon became a free-for-all business, and I had a boarding school full of clients.

Looking back now, I realise I was rather naïve; I could have made a small fortune! But I so wanted to belong somewhere, to be accepted, I would have done anything.

Many of the boys came from broken or dysfunctional families, from which emotionally dependent relationships began to form. Reflecting back, I now realise that putting a bunch of kids with desperate emotional and physical needs together in a house without additional parental support is a recipe for disaster. And for some it was, but for many it became the only real home they had.

By this time I was a very self-conscious teenager, and had become even more anxious about my personal life, and particularly about my identity as a boy with so many mixed-up emotions. I was needy, desperately lonely, and I would have done anything for friendship. I was also in the thick of puberty, and masturbation had become a friend. It was a release, but lust had also been awoken and my hormones were raging. I had no dad, no older brothers or good male role model. I was alone trying to figure it all out. Or was I? No, I was in boarding school surrounded by lots of other men!

There was one particular senior in boarding school that had taken me under his wing. I often did small jobs for him and liked him because he was kind to me.

As you would expect, smoking was forbidden in the school,

but that didn't stop a good number of the guys doing it in secret. He was one of them. One afternoon after study break, he asked me to come with him to where the smokers used to go. It was just outside the property, down a steep embankment under tall growth by a riverbed.

My heart raced, for this was dangerous and the consequences of being caught were severe – a good hiding from the principal. And if caught more than once, there was a risk of being expelled. But I was an accomplice now as I sat there next to him on the bank. It was more like lying down, for the embankment that we sat on was steep, but well out of sight. I assumed he trusted me, because he had invited me to go with him, and I had grown to trust him over the months. So that afternoon I found myself confiding in him about my childhood and the sexual abuse back on the farm.

His immediate reaction was one of disbelief, which quickly turned to blaming me for being an attention-seeking junior. I was consumed with fear, expecting the worst; expecting him to tell the whole school. I would have done anything to prevent that from happening. I was so scared.

He looked at me, but I couldn't look at him; I was too embarrassed, too scared; too vulnerable. I had thought I would be safe, for he had trusted me enough to see him smoking. Then the next thing I knew, he moved over to where I was lying, pulled his trousers down and exposed himself.

'Take it,' he said. 'Come on, show me what you did on the farm, show me that it's the truth, or I will…'

I did show him. Why, I do not know. Maybe out of fear, or from a warped and desperate desire to be loved. Was this love? And so began another abusive relationship with another male figure I looked up to.

How stupid was I to have thought that he could help, or even wanted to? What would happen if he told on me? After all that I had been through, I wasn't looking for attention; I just wanted to tell someone – but now this. I didn't want this.

He would come and fetch me, which wasn't strange, for lots of juniors had to do jobs during the first year of school. So nobody suspected anything, especially this. It went on for a good six months. I got used to it, and I came not to mind it anymore.

How could I come to like someone for something that was so wrong? Was it because it filled my need for love and affection? Was it fear, fear of rejection? Or was it lust? Somewhere in all of this I had become a young man; and then I thought, there are lots of other boys going through pretty much the same hormonal development as me, so maybe this is just how it is.

CHAPTER 7
I'M GAY
+ + +

I went back home to *Ouma's* one weekend. I was in a bad mood because I wanted to go out with some mates in the village, but Ma had forbidden me to go out dressed as I was – in some black flared trousers.

'You are not going out in those,' I was told in no uncertain terms.

'It's my life and I will dress however I want,' was my reply. I was angry; so angry that I went back to my room, cut the trousers up in to little bits and then threw them all over her bedroom. If I wasn't going to wear them, nobody was.

As I walked past Ma, telling her exactly what I thought, she suddenly sidestepped me. We were now face to face. 'Ennrich, are there any gay activities going on at boarding school?' she asked. It was like she winded me with her words. I couldn't speak, not a word. So I just walked away. What! How did she know?

It took me a long time to get an answer to that question but when I did, I was horrified. It transpired that on 'that day', the day I was invited down to the smoker's den when it all happened with him, we were observed. The spot was directly across the river from a grand estate and, unbeknown to us, a fellow pupil from the same school was playing out in his garden with some binoculars and he saw the whole thing unfold.

The news travelled quickly to his parents, who knew my aunt, my ma, the teachers and the principal. Soon everybody knew, but no one ever said a word to me about it. Why did they never come and speak to me directly about what they had been told or what they had seen? It was simply perceived as if what happened that day on the embankment with him was all with my consent. Was it? Little did they know about the ongoing abusive relationship! Regardless of whether I consented to it or not, how was what they had been told about it OK? I was fourteen and the senior was eighteen; I did not consent. So how could Ma ask me this question, and how did the little that she did know now make me gay? My conclusion was that I must be gay, then!

In the aftermath, I decided to come clean with Ma and tell her about the abuse within the 'family' all those years ago in the farmhouse. So I wrote a letter to her and included that I thought I might be gay. Not that I really knew what that word meant. It was just a word that I had been called so many times before, and was clutching for my true identity.

Later, we cried together. She was so shocked, and blamed herself for not being there for me at the time. Ma did what any parent would have done; she tried in her way to fix it. But she never could. The whole episode left me feeling awful for writing to her at all. I had made her feel bad about her absence and made her suffer in the present for those historic events. It was actually all about me. I feared losing yet another parent. I was sinking fast.

Six months into it, I just couldn't cope anymore. I couldn't handle the relationship, no matter how wrong or abusive it was, and I certainly couldn't handle the emotions involved. Part of me loved and liked him, while another side of me was emotionally incapable and way too immature to handle the sexual side of it all. He was kissing me now, as if I was his! I was never asked to enter into this, it just happened, and now he wanted more and more. I took some solace from knowing he was going to leave school soon, but then what?

The mental and emotional turmoil drove me to thinking a lot about dying, just giving up on life. Killing myself seemed like a good way out of all the mess. I hated life, my life and myself. The thought gradually increased in its appeal to me and I started to plan for it. I started asking around for painkillers, as most kids had some access to their own tablets. Very discreetly I gathered a good handful. Then one day, at the time when we could take a nap before supper, I took them all at once and went to lie down in the bedroom I shared with the other boys.

Henry, one of the boys who shared with me, came into the room some time later. Apparently he had peeled an orange and when he went to throw the peel away noticed the empty packets in the bin. He raised the alarm and sent for help. The very same teacher that was meant to keep an eye on me came and carried me to his room and then phoned the doctor. Through the haze I could hear him reading off the names of what was in the bin.

A concoction of lukewarm milk mixed with saltwater was brought up from the kitchen and I was forced to drink it until I vomited. And so I did. Through the gagging, the heaving and clutching, I cried. Not just for this, but for being caught. I had wanted to die, not this embarrassment, not to be saved by them, and particularly by him, the very teacher who was to 'look out for me'. I didn't trust him; he was just there to spy on me and to report back to the family. I didn't trust anyone anymore.

That night I slept in the sickbay. The next morning, I woke up with him, the senior, leaning over me. How did he get in? We were face to face when I opened my eyes. I was frozen solid with fear. All he said was, 'I'm sorry.' He kissed me and left the room. I tried to sleep but my mind was racing. Did he know I had told the teachers about him? I eventually drifted off.

The next day the questions started. I was so scared. I didn't want the senior to get into trouble. He was in the middle of preparing for his final exams and I didn't want him to be expelled for me telling on him. Oh, if I had only shut up, endured it, hung in there and kept up with it, he would have left anyway. He would have left school, left me, and none of this would have been known.

I begged the teachers to lie about it. 'Please tell him that another prefect or senior saw us and blew the whistle. Please don't tell him I told you. I was meant to die, it wasn't meant to come out; it wasn't supposed to happen this way.'

The doctor never came and Ma couldn't come that day either. It was the most terrible of terrible days.

I slept in the sickbay again, or at least I tried to. My head was so full of the stuff that had happened and my heart raced continually. What had they told him? What did they say about what had happened to me? Over and over I replayed it in my mind. And to this day I don't know what was said between them all.

What followed was a year of appointments with a psychologist at Tygerberg Hospital in Cape Town. The idea was to help me come to terms with 'it' – my sexuality and sexual orientation. Throughout my time in therapy we never talked about why I had these same-sex feelings. It became far easier to simply make peace with it and accept it: I was gay. No alternatives were offered to me, just 'make peace and accept it'. This was my new sexuality and identity.

I recall thinking, 'there must be an alternative to this' and then suppressing the question. After all, these were medical professionals, and if they had no alternatives to my gender issues and sexuality, who did? So there I was, left with no answers to my fundamental questions about where my past experiences fitted in to all this. Were they saying I was therefore born this way? Was 'making peace and accepting it' really the only way forward?

CHAPTER 8
SCHOOL'S OUT
+ + +

Back at school everyone looked at me strangely and treated me differently. It was as if they all knew something, but I didn't know what. Sometime later one boy had the guts to ask me if I had something wrong with my genitals. What? They had no clue. Kids can be so cruel. It was better that they did not know the truth.

The attempt to kill myself alienated me even more. People kept their distance. The few friends I had left were ones in similar abusive relationships at the school, but even they were keeping their distance for fear of being exposed.

We had to go to church on Sundays. One week as I was walking down the path in the churchyard, I saw my maths teacher speaking to the local minister. As their eyes caught mine, their conversation went quiet. All I felt was judgement and rejection. Was I just being sensitive or was it the truth? Were they even talking about me at all? Or was it my guilt and shame that made me feel this way? No matter the reason, I can still remember the look of utter disgust on their faces.

My situation wasn't dealt with particularly well, but it wasn't until more recently that I actually thought about why the police and social services had not been involved. Maybe the school was trying to save face. Perhaps they feared that having negative publicity would ruin their reputation, and that of the parents of the senior, who were esteemed, well-to-do farmers in the district. Or had they already decided for me that I was gay, so there was no issue; it was just how the gays behaved? I have to rest in the fact that it was just the way things were back then in South Africa. It doesn't make it right; but it explains some things.

School life continued and some of the boys were increasingly curious about their own sexuality and wanted to experiment, which led to many 'one-night stands'. I began to seek them out, looking for an encounter. The more alone and estranged I felt, the more desperate I became for love, touch, affection and friendship. I guess it was my way of dealing with the pain, anger and shame. Over time it had become known that I was easy, and more and more boys and men followed. It was a deadly, downward spiral that threatened to completely engulf me.

As you can imagine, this also had an impact on my family, especially my younger brother. He had been at the same school throughout all these events, and he began to have an increasingly hard time, especially with my lifestyle, as it had become more and more known that I was both gay and easy. One day we had a massive fight in the showers and he tried to punch me, lashing out in frustration. I got the upper hand but had not fully understood that his extreme anger towards me was rooted in him being mocked and bullied about me. Ma thought it was best for him to move schools again which he did, and I stayed on for another year or so.

The downward spiral continued. Wednesday afternoons were free at boarding school, so we used them to go into town to buy personal necessities or to meet our friends. It was on one of those trips out that I met a young man from another school. He just happened to attend the same party as me one weekend and we started a relationship.

I used to sneak out of boarding school to see him. He would ride past on his motorbike, sounding the horn in a certain way as a cue for me to be picked up. Nobody knew about us. We usually went to his parents' place for the evening because he was an only child and slept in an extension away from his parents' house. His room was full of porn magazines. It was the first time I'd been exposed to such explicit pornography and our relationship, if you can call it that, was more about getting rid of sexual tension than anything else. It lasted about a year, and alongside it there was a steady stream of sexual experimentation happening at boarding school as well.

Soon after I was sixteen, another senior guy came and asked me for a 'massage'. Yeah, right! Those types of question were codes for all sorts. It had a 'happy ending' for him but was about to go badly for me. Afterwards, he went back to the same teacher – the one who had taught me how to make a bed, my extended family member, the one who got me to vomit when my stomach was full of tablets, that very same teacher – and told him I had pushed it too far.

It was all a set-up. It seems I had become a huge liability for the school and its reputation. They had no control over me, or should I say 'over it'! I was also smoking and part of a group of outlaws that were into guys, smoking and booze. It was time to remove the liability.

The principal called me into his office, and I was surprised to find my ma already sat there. I had no idea what was coming, but he basically asked me to leave the school. To make it easier for me he explained they had already spoken to the head of another school and it had been arranged for me to transfer there to complete my education. Just like that.

All this was a direct result of my sexuality and its expression in a very conservative community. It was simply no longer going to be tolerated! I was being expelled without it being called that, and ostracised by some of my close friends, because their sexuality was being questioned on account of their connection to me. They were being deemed guilty by association, which needed sorting out, and what better way than to remove the problem – me.

Ma tried to defend me as best she could. I can clearly remember her saying to the headmaster that this was no way to handle things, and to be sure that this day would come back to revisit him! What she really meant was that chasing me away was not going to resolve the issue. And that was it. It was all very civilised and I left; or should I say, I was snuck out of the back door.

The practicalities meant that we had to move to a new town and a new boarding school, and Ma moved house again to be closer to all three of us.

The new boarding school was great. The schoolteachers and parents knew a few things about me, but had a certain kindness and grace towards me, and I managed to continue my sexual experimentation unhindered.

Academically I was all over the place. I dropped three of my major subjects – chemistry, accounting and maths – and took on three new ones: economics, business economics and agricultural science. I'd no interest left in school or an academic career, these subjects just seemed like a more palatable way to fill my classroom hours. My only aim was to just get it over and done with.

Relationships were mostly superficial due to the lack of time or ability to build deeper ones, and my inadequacy to sustain them. I would find myself either completely falling for or fooling around with guys, or suffering the fear of rejection by not being good enough for their crowd. The anxiety around relationships completely occupied and dominated my headspace.

Sex had become a commodity, like trading toys, or buying something at the shop. Boys had to know that I was available, so I gently pushed for it, for sex. But it was love and affection, acceptance and physical touch that I craved more than anything. I would have done anything for it. The never-ending search for love was insatiable. What lengths I went to for some attention. I was desperate, spent and wasted.

Drama class at school was a welcome release, an opportunity to express some of the emotions that were locked up inside me. There I met a girl. I really liked her. She was beautiful and came from a good home, with a solid Christian upbringing. She was very clever and interesting. What's more, she liked me and I was OK with it. She was kind to me. Sometimes I thought she was being kind just because she pitied me. But that was just me. I couldn't understand it; I didn't know what to do or how to handle it when someone showed me real love or affection. I also didn't know why I was so drawn to her. But I felt safe with her.

Her family took me in, which was a great relief after spending weekend after weekend in boarding school. Her dad was a wine farmer, her ma and her two older sisters were all into medicine. Weekends on their farm were great, but did remind me of the past we had lost. I sometimes sat with her family in church too. It was the main Dutch Reformed Church where her parents were members. They were so kind to me, and I felt like I belonged somewhere for the first time ever. I did try to take her to my house, but her ma wouldn't have it. I didn't understand why. I did love her and I wouldn't have done anything to hurt her. Our relationship had become physical, but we never had sex; well, it stopped just short of it. She was a Christian girl who loved Jesus and what we did had already been one step too far for her.

We loved each other very much and became very close. We had become close enough for me to trust her, to trust her enough to tell her about the abuse and all the stuff from my past. She cried for me, for my hurt. It felt good to have someone who cared enough to feel with me and for me.

On one occasion, Ma came to fetch me from their farm. Her ma invited mine into the house and took her aside for a chat. We left shortly after and I got the feeling that Ma had been asked in a polite kind of way to discourage the relationship. I was really annoyed. Once again, I was left feeling not good enough. They were obviously aiming higher than a guy like me for their daughter; someone higher than my class, my breeding, or my sort, whatever sort that was. I just took it as more rejection.

High school finally came to an end, and with it the relationship. But we had not given in to the background gossip between our ma's, which was a little personal triumph.

Just how I got through school I will never know. I had read my textbooks once or twice and then sat my finals. I just wanted to finish. But the truth was, I was scared of it all coming to an end. So many familiar things were about to finish, and I was going into the army next to do my national service. I didn't want to go, but we had to. Two years of national service was compulsory for all white South African men. The alternative was two years in prison or detention barracks, under the surveillance of the military police. I met all the physical criteria, was the right age and fit enough. Therefore I had to go and defend our great institutions, like family, church, school and state – the very institutions that I felt had failed me. And, of course, the shame of not going would always have been too much for a damaged soul like me to bear. So, I complied.

CHAPTER 9
IN THE ARMY NOW
+ + +

The long hot summer between me finishing school and entering the army was the last one we spent together as a family. I remember it well, for both positive and negative reasons.

It started badly. One weekend while back at Ma's, she decided to share with me that my brother had found the letter I had written four years earlier just before my suicide attempt, the one about the abuse on the farm. And not just recently, he had found it all those years ago! I was horrified. That meant he had known about it all this time and never mentioned it. Was there so little relationship left between us that he never felt we could have an honest conversation about it?

Ma went on to tell me that he had been so angry about what had happened to me, he wanted to go back to the farm and take revenge on my behalf. He had ranted and raged about going back and killing our stepbrother. He was only thirteen at the time, of course, and processing it all must have been very hard for him. In a strange kind of way it comforted me that he cared enough to have wanted to do that for me; not that I believe killing anyone can ever make you feel better.

The next time I saw him, things were very strange. I was half-angry at him for knowing all these years and not saying anything, and half-ashamed of him knowing at all. All I could say was, 'Tell me, brother, did our stepbrother do any of that sort of thing to you?'

'No,' he responded.

Relieved at his answer, we left it there. There was so much that I wanted to say, but the weight of my shame and embarrassment was so heavy, I couldn't go there. And neither could he.

I now understood why being together at boarding school had not been easy for him. It now made sense why he had been so angry and why he had lashed out at me that time. He had read the letter and then had his own share of conflicting emotions to navigate, and to top it all, my reputation must have hung over him like a dark cloud. So, guilt, shame and lack of communication ate away at our relationship.

Some relief from that bad start to the summer came as we all headed off to *Ouma's* house at the coast. She had the house built after she retired from farming, some fifteen years earlier, and we had spent most of our summer holidays there ever since. It was a massive house that fronted the beach not far from the high-tide line. That was the house where I had always felt most at home. We spent many a happy day catching up with all the friends we had got to know there over the years.

In amongst it all, I remember the few nerve-racking days just before my exam results arrived. The results were published in one of the major newspapers, so everyone knew how you had done! The night before, we all stayed up as the paper was delivered in the early hours of the morning. Tentatively, I scanned the columns, and what a relief it was to find my name among the passes. Phew! A serious celebration party followed, with a bonfire on the beach and plenty of booze, drugs and making out with as many people as possible. My ma knew about this. I was self-medicating to cope, even though there are no solutions at the bottom of any bottle!

But then the holidays ended. This last summer of freedom and carefree living gave way to the serious responsibility of serving my country.

When the call up came, we had the opportunity to request the type of regiment we would prefer to serve in. There was no guarantee it would be granted, of course, but I got lucky. I had requested enlistment in the medical regiment which was based in the north of the country, 1,500 kilometres away from everything and everybody I knew, and I was enrolled as a medical orderly.

Our intake consisted of 2,600 young men. There were 1,700 post-high school students like me and about 900 post-graduate medical and dental students.

The train, with its first load of young troops, left Cape Town and headed north on its three-day journey towards Pretoria. I'd boarded dressed in navy and white pinstripe Bermuda shorts and a military T-shirt emblazoned with the rank of an admiral in the Navy. What was I thinking? My hair was long, and dyed red too. As you'd expect, my attire provoked a lot of attention – and I wondered why!

The military police guarded the train closely – particularly when it stopped – which it did at virtually every small town and village on its 1,500-kilometre journey, picking up troops at each one. We had to lock down the windows, shutters and doors before every station, because we were a large group of white boys and therefore a potential target for any anti-government, anti-military or anti-white group in those awful days of apartheid.

I was ordered to carry the rifle of one of the military police officers on the train. This unexpected privilege brought me free access to everywhere he went, so I got to see every compartment and met everyone on the train. He introduced me as his 'fitting'; no name, just as his 'fitting'. It was a bit of an ambiguous term, but the guys made of it what they wanted, and I liked all the attention it brought me. Here I was being paraded up and down the train as a well-groomed, 'fit' young guy. I loved it.

Looking back, it's ironic that 'fitting' was the last thing I did. I didn't know who I was, who I was meant to be, or where I fitted. All I know is that I submitted to the process along with the rest of that fledgling army of raw recruits, and waited to see what would happen next.

Free from the restrictions of being accountable to anyone, this is when I well and truly 'came out of the closet'; I was loud and proud. Free from the watchful eyes of parents, teachers, family, friends or church folk, I started to do anything to get noticed. I was no longer ashamed of who I was, and wanted the world to know. I was on a mission to prove something. If too many days went by without me getting some attention, I would dress up by putting ox-blood shoe polish on my face as make-up and parade myself around the barracks to attract some guys. How desperate!

I discovered there were lots of guys experimenting with their sexuality, some out of loneliness, and others out of boredom and frustration, but all struggling to some extent with their identity. It was crazy and fun at the same time. Those who didn't know who they were became a challenge for me; they became someone with something to conquer. I had one thing on my mind, and that was to sleep around with as many as possible, in the hope of finding someone who might love me for longer than a night. I was desperate for love.

I tried to do it as sweetly as possible; I didn't want to offend but it was offensive to some. And I suffered the consequences by giving them lots of opportunities to bully me and for me to take offence. But I reasoned to myself that it was just the cross I had to bear.

Many nights in the dormitory of about fifty guys, my leg would be gently kicking the bed as I slept – something that was still happening all those years later – so they would come and flip my bed with me in it. Even though we were a platoon and supposedly responsible for each other, I was different and treated as an annoying embarrassment by some of them. Sometimes they wouldn't bother getting me up for roll call in the morning, just so I could get picked on. I hated this part of the army and being treated this way. All I wanted was to belong, but this stuff made me want to run from it. After all, I hadn't asked to join; I'd been forced to spend the next two years of my life there.

Fortunately there were others of my kind there, and I soon met a bunch of guys that were also gay. We realised that if we ganged up, there was some sort of safety in numbers. They became my friends, my troops in this war inside the war. We were comrades, all struggling to exist, never mind coexist with the straight guys. We hung out together and sneaked out of the camp some nights to visit the local gay clubs in the city. We did it for relief, just to be ourselves and not to pretend anymore and, of course, to score a one-night stand.

A very close friend in the group had a Jaguar sports car in which we could just drive in and out of the camp. Nobody questioned us because they never expected an eighteen-year-old to be driving such an expensive car, so even the security guys ignored it. His dad was a famous plastic surgeon in Johannesburg. He was a very attractive young man who had already had some 'work' done on his face, organised by his dad. I found it weird that his father would let him have plastic surgery. Was he not handsome enough or good enough to be his son? Why did he need a nose job? We were good friends, so I never asked.

We had a very good, open friendship and I use to tell him what guys I fancied, to which he was generally unresponsive. Then one day I found myself in an awkward situation with him and things changed. He called me over to the part of the dormitory where he slept. There was a big old cupboard down there with the door standing open. I walked up to it and peeked in. There he stood, naked, looking at me in a longing way. I had not expected this. He was my friend, not my lover.

Things were never the same between us after that, because I could not give him what he wanted. Actually, I did not have it to give. You see, it was much easier to sleep with a stranger than with a real friend. I couldn't put into words what I felt deep down inside, or maybe I was just afraid to explain myself to him for fear of being misunderstood. It broke my heart. I could have sex with so many others, but was completely unable to be intimate with a friend that I really loved.

Anyway, life went on and there were lots of other mates to hang out with. We did life at 100 miles an hour, life that revolved around drugs, booze and clubbing. Somewhere in between we fitted in our army life, our primary mission always being to get back into camp without getting caught by the guards after a long night's partying. That became a military exercise in itself!

CHAPTER 10
DEFILED AND RELEASED
+ + +

A weekend pass was coming up, which also happened to be on my birthday. I sensed a celebration coming but couldn't go back to Cape Town as it was too far away. However, Jay, another good friend, who lived in Pretoria, invited me to go home with him. He was a qualified hairdresser who had worked in a salon before being called up for national service. So we planned to go clubbing each night and for him to work on the Saturday to boost his income.

We drank a lot that Friday evening, even before getting to the club. It was 10:30 and the vibe was picking up. After some shots at the bar, bought by a number of interested parties, we ended up on the dance floor. Having drinks bought by a stranger was not a new experience but this was also dangerous, for it could have been laced with all sorts of drugs. More booze, more dancing. Someone handed me a bottle of 'poppers' and as I was about to take a hit, a body bumped into me causing the whole container of amyl nitrate to empty on my shirt. The wave of fumes hit me hard. I was so high and drunk, all I can remember was smiling and the others laughing at me, or with me.

In amongst our friends from the camp, there was also this stranger. I think it was he who handed me the bottle of 'poppers' in the first place. He came and danced with me, very close-up; I could tell he was into me. The night went on and it became one big blur and I can't remember when I lost the rest of the crowd, but I found myself being carried up some stairs and I remember hearing a key turn in a door lock. The next moment I was on a carpet somewhere, facedown with the weight of something like a heavy piece of wooden furniture resting on my neck. I tried to resist but he had my hands behind my back as he stripped me, and without saying a word he forced himself on me and raped me. I must have passed out at some stage but woke up the next morning next to him.

My body was in such pain. He wanted more. What! I kept my composure and told him I had to go to the salon where my friend worked, and that I would be in trouble if I didn't arrive. I had no clue where I was in this strange city. I was scared and knew I just had to get out of there and away from him. He dropped me at the shopping mall and awkwardly I said goodbye to him. I never saw him again.

I walked through the mall acutely aware of my pain, shame and anger. How could I have been so stupid as to allow him to defile me like that? How dare he do that to me, without even asking me? Did he think just because I had passed out that he had my consent? I was fuming with anger as I arrived at the salon.

Jay was with a client when I walked into the shop. He nodded in my direction and I could tell that he had been worried about me. I was very aware of the pain my body was in and that I was still dressed in my clothes from the night before. So I spent the Saturday tidying up in the shop, sweeping floors, sorting towels, magazines and drinks for the clients, partially out of guilt, for making him worried.

When we eventually caught up, I couldn't tell Jay what had happened, I felt so guilty. All I could say was that I was sorry for causing him worry. I shelved the memories of that terrible night, pushing them to the very back of my mind, and just kept going. Life was not going to wait for me to catch up, I just had to grab it and press on. It's amazing how robust we are in certain situations. Well, I suppose I had a choice. I could have gone to the authorities, which at the time seemed insane given that I willingly went to a gay bar the night before and hooked up with a complete stranger. It was also a known fact at the time that the authorities had very little insight into or compassion for male rape or sexual violation. Perhaps it was my own guilt, pride, fear or shame that prevented me from going to seek help. I chose to settle for this: that it was the only thing I was good for. From then on, my behaviour, my self-esteem, even the way I dressed, were purposely directly towards drawing more attention to myself. I was not going to be the victim. But no matter how much I denied it, I was. Outwardly I looked confident and full of bravado, even sexually arrogant, but deep inside I was deeply insecure, scared and lonely. I felt dead. I hated myself, my own body, but desperately fed on any sexual attention that came my way. For me, sex equalled love.

On the wider political front, the conflict on our south-west border with Angola and some of the other neighbouring countries had come to an end. So, thankfully, that reduced the likelihood of me having to take part in any direct military action during my time in the army. But I was reminded constantly that according to the Geneva Convention I was first a soldier and second a medical orderly, so I may be called upon to fight for my country. How could I ever have killed another human being? Thankfully it was never required of me, for which I am eternally grateful.

When my six months' basic and medical training came to an

end we were posted to units all over the country. I was transferred back to Cape Town, sad to leave my new friends. We vowed to keep in touch but rarely did.

I was now posted to the psychiatric ward of the military hospital, another whole new world for me. It was a world that quickly fascinated me. The ward was filled with guys struggling with serious life issues, many from a physical trauma, but the deep damage was in their mind and soul. We handled a lot of casualty evacuations, physical injuries and those suffering post-traumatic stress disorder, caused by emotional and psychological strain from the war and post-war situations. Many had 'cracked up'; they had lost their minds as a result of what they had been through and what they had seen.

I seemed to cope well in this new world and started to really enjoy the job. I liked working with patients and helping those damaged souls along the road to recovery. I can remember thinking that it felt good to mean something to someone, other than just knowing them for sex.

Sadly, that didn't last for long. There was one particular patient who struggled with his identity and had tried to overdose, resulting in him being placed on our ward. We got on well – too well. The ward was near the barracks where I lived and he came to visit me one evening, and soon made a move indicating that he wanted to sleep with me. So we did. What was I thinking? I could have ended up in so much trouble for that. But 'what the hell', I reasoned, we were both government property at the time. And what did it matter, anyway? I was obviously still good for one thing, sex.

Midway through my time in the military hospital, I became interested in my roots on my father's side and started to do some genealogical exploration. I tracked my real dad's records down, which also led me to his second wife, the one he had eventually moved on to from Ma. I was intrigued and managed to find her in the local directory. Believe it or not, she lived in the suburb adjoining where I was based.

It took all the courage I had to call her, but she was delighted to hear from me, so we arranged to meet in a restaurant near to where we both lived. It was very strange to be reopening, or maybe I should say opening, this chapter of my life. I assumed I had never met her before but I sensed I had, probably at Dad's funeral all those years ago. I was only seven at the time so couldn't say for certain.

It was a little uncomfortable to start off with because we had no obvious starting point to pick up from. She and Dad had been married only seven months before he tragically died, but she had obviously known him longer than that. So she was a route to information about Dad for me, a man I had no memory of ever meeting. As the evening came to an end, I was eager to see her again. I even dared to say that I would like to get to know more about my dad, even though I knew it was going to be tough for her.

Sadly, I never saw her again. She didn't answer any of my calls or reply to my letters. Eventually I received a short letter from my grandmother on my father's side saying that it had all been too upsetting for her to talk about him as she was still hurting. She also explained that early in their relationship my dad had once said to her that maybe his children – meaning my brother and I – would one day find out through her who he really was. That had haunted her mind. Had he therefore suspected he would die? Anyway, it was just all too much for her.

Now I was the one left wondering. Did this imply that he had wanted to see us, and couldn't or wasn't allowed to at the time? The only other person I could ask was Ma, but she either got angry or cried when I raised the subject of him with her. So I was left feeling hopeless about ever knowing what had really happened. In the end, I had to accept that I would never know, so left it there. No matter how many questions I had about my dad, answered or unanswered, he was still dead, and knowing about him could never replace knowing him. My search for him, and for answers, had an impact on others who, in their own search for peace, had their own struggles coming to terms with his death. I was still looking for that missing piece; for him. What I really needed was peace in my own heart.

For the last period of my national service I was asked to go and work at the Army Medical Headquarters based in the City Bowl area. This was a very exciting prospect, as all the action was in the city centre and it would have provided me with a great lifestyle. However, the job required me to have a driving licence. So I set about getting the test passed, but it entailed me taking a huge truck through the busy city traffic and I was so scared, I failed. On reporting back I told my superior, a brigadier, that my dad had died in a car accident and that I was therefore too scared to drive. I felt pathetic, but it was the truth.

She was kind to me and decided to post me instead to a smaller clinic at a nearby airforce base for the final months of my national service. I got on well with the staff and took the decision to talk to the resident psychologist about all the 'stuff' in my life. I told him as much as I could, including that I was gay and depressed. After three months of sessions, he came to the conclusion that I just had to make peace with it all. I was depressed because I was fighting it, so 'making peace and accepting it' was the answer. I had heard this before and not been able to, so why would it be any different this time? Why could I not just accept it? And what on earth did he mean by 'making peace' with it? On reflection I was looking to another adult for guidance, yet was left with the question 'what's wrong with me?' No one asked 'what's happened to you?' I was left as restless and confused as ever.

Then all of a sudden, my two-year contract of national service was cut short. The government decided that compulsory national service would be phased out altogether in favour of a voluntary one, and it was implemented straight away. Those were days of major change in South Africa. It was just before the release of Nelson Mandela, which was about to usher in massive political and structural changes to the whole nation. So my two years became eighteen months and I was out.

My brother, who was enrolled into doing his military service a year after me, had also been having a bad time. He had been adversely affected by some of the things his time with the Infantry had exposed him to. He saw death, conflict and trauma up close, and it deeply affected him. He too was released early, and by this quirk of fate we both ended up returning home to Ma prematurely.

CHAPTER 11
HAIR SCHOOL
+ + +

Our sudden homecoming was a shock to Ma. She hadn't expected me back just yet and wasn't expecting my brother for another year! So a few rocky weeks followed. We were all a bit disorientated and in very different seasons of life. And for my part, I still had no idea what I wanted to do with my life from a career point of view.

Things slowly clarified, in no little part because of an inheritance we had been left following our father's death.

We had known for a while that our dad had left us a small sum of money in his estate. But only now did we learn that if our ma had not to put a claim in against his estate following his death, we would have received nothing. He had died intestate, so never actually made provision for us in a will, which left me thinking, 'Gee, thanks, Dad, for not providing for us yet again!' But Ma's intervention secured a sum for my brother and I, equivalent to about £2,000 each in today's money. It was to be released to us by the court when we became twenty-one, and I was just about there. Although it wasn't much, it was enough to carry me through college and I am now very grateful that I was enabled to finish college with no debt at all. And that college was hair school in Cape Town.

So now I was now a freshman in college and after surviving the initial *'doop'* (initiation) things had settled down nicely. I shared a room with a guy from Namibia who studied marketing. I made it my mission to let as many fellow students in residence on campus as possible know that I was gay and proud. I was in my element! My surroundings and fellow classmates were fully compatible with my gay status, and I even made it my business to help a few of them come to terms with their 'confused' identities.

We had so much fun. Twenty years of suppressed creativity now had ample opportunity to blossom to the full. I really excelled in the hair world. It not only gave me the opportunity to express my sexual identity, but also to fulfil my longing to be close to people, to be loved and accepted. I soon realised that the better I became at doing hair, the more leeway I had with my clients, which in turn gave me even greater opportunity to express my creativity, and that brought me even closer to them – or so I thought. On reflection, I think I was earning some love the hard way. It's called a performance-driven reward. Nevertheless, in hairdressing I found a safe place to be.

I did well in all my exams, especially the practical ones, and on top of that I was nominated to represent the hair and cosmetology department on the student council. What a privilege and opportunity. I found myself in leadership – unbelievable! It made me feel very important having this responsibility, but always scared me a little. Expectations were high in what was still an all-white environment where arrogance, prejudice and the fear of others always lingered just below the surface. Yet this responsibility satisfied my desperate search for approval to some degree, so I faced the fear and did it anyway.

I soon made good friends there. Being outgoing, I attracted liberated, likeminded people, and we became a force to be reckoned with. We were never aggressive in our approach, but at the same time, no pushovers. This amazing bunch included the daughter of a high-ranking politician, some artists, and a few from prominent farming families. We were a mixture of nationalities too. We never called ourselves anything, but very organically stood together for what we believed in and gained subtle momentum for others to gravitate towards. I was their 'leader'.

It was at this time that I entered my first long-term relationship. We met at a club one evening. He was a fashion designer, eight years my senior. He was a great guy who was experienced in the gay scene. It felt so good to be loved by someone. He was very well-connected in the fashion world and, being a student stylist myself, we explored the many avenues of furthering my career.

At one point, we requested application forms for me to work for the internationally acclaimed company, Toni & Guy, but I decided not to pursue it at the time. I was now in a settled relationship, felt loved and it was too much to give up.

Our relationship was challenged on many fronts: there was the age factor to start with, and then me being a student while he was a working man. We lived apart too. I remained in a college residence while he lived in a flat in Camps Bay, a very affluent suburb of Cape Town. Consequently, we only saw each other some evenings and at weekends.

Without going into detail here, I should mention that I found it impossible to have a truly intimate or sexual relationship with him. I found it impossible to 'go there', and even though it's hard to admit, I was dysfunctional in bed. He was so patient with me, but the fear of intimacy and my serious reservations about sex placed a huge strain on our relationship. Was it because of the army experience? I just could not figure it out. So we ended up in a situation where we loved each other, but I couldn't express it through sex. This frustration eventually got to him. On reflection I had learnt a continuing pattern of earning love through sex.

Now to love and give of myself physically, giving everything, was far too frightening. I couldn't make myself that vulnerable. I struggled with trust as a foundation from which to willingly give of myself in order to be intimate.

A year in, he met somebody else and cheated on me. He was very open and honest about it. But here I was again; most of the male role models in my life had either left, died, cheated or abused me, so what else should I expect? It ended our relationship. I felt angry, betrayed, and disappointed in him and myself. My inadequacy had contributed to us falling apart, and I knew I was partially to blame. Blaming others or myself did not help, it only added more stress and created more guilt. I felt so guilty. I needed help, but where could I go?

During my second year of college, the campus relocated some departments, including hair and cosmetology, to another suburb in Cape Town. We moved from a very affluent, white upper-middle class area to an extremely poor area. I had been approached to take on the position as chair of the student council at the new campus, so that was a great incentive for me.

We all had to get new housing because of the relocation, as the college residences we had previously occupied were too remote from the new campus. So I teamed up with a gay classmate and moved into a private residence within walking distance from the new campus. We got on well. Our landlords lived in and provided meals, did our washing and all the basic household chores, which made the transition easy.

He often joined me on weekends because his family were a two-hour flight away in Namibia. Chris and I were just friends. He suffered from dyslexia, which I helped him with by studying out loud so that he could listen and learn at the same time as me. He could actually retain the work better this way. In return his friendship eased the pain of my loneliness after what felt like the 100th disappointment and broken relationship. After the break-up I had multiple one-night stands; they were my 'drug of choice', you might say. It seemed casual sex was do-able but never sex in a relationship; that was too intimate. I was still searching for love, which typically ended up with more disappointment than fulfilment. So I was so glad for the pure friendship of my housemate.

We partied on a weekend, getting drunk and very stoned on anything we could get our hands on. My dead father's money came in handy for this too!

Our studies soon finished and Chris returned to Windhoek, Namibia, where he had a job waiting for him. I was so sad to see him go. It was then that I moved in with Jo. He was another good friend who lived in a flat even closer to Cape Town city centre where we became part of the arty clique, frequenting theatres, clubs and parties. We were living the 'high-life'.

Jo had a very bold personality and brimmed with confidence. Like me he was from farming stock, and had studied opera at the University of Cape Town. At first we enjoyed a good life and all that the beautiful city of Cape Town and its glorious surroundings had to offer. We spent most of our time together, eating out, entertaining friends. We even made a couple of trips to his parents' farm on the Orange River. They were grape farmers and he was their only son. It was a lovely piece of land, and even had an open gemstone mine on it with the mineral rights belonging to the family. He was very kind and became instrumental in me finding my first job in Cape Town.

There was a wonderful salon in the centre of Cape Town on Green Market Square. It was one of the top ten best hair salons in South Africa and I really wanted to work there. One day as we passed it, I stopped and was musing about how amazing it would be to work at a place like that. Suddenly Jo grabbed me by the shoulder and said, 'Well, let's go in and ask them for a job!' With a bit of gentle nudging, he pushed me through the doors and up to reception. I was edgy because I'd no appointment, nor was there a notice in the window advertising for vacancies. But there we were.

I asked to speak with the manager, and by some miracle it was the owner sat at the reception desk. So with every ounce of boldness I could muster, I politely said, 'I would really love to work here if you have any openings. I've just finished my studies at hair school, and want to start my career in an amazing salon like this.' From the look on his face, I knew I had caught him by surprise. But he was taken by my boldness, and after some conversation, the answer was 'yes' and I started the following week.

It was an incredible place to work. The staff were a real international bunch. The bosses were Dutch and Chinese, my colleagues German, Czech, British and Xhosa South African; black and white all working together. I was the only one from Boer stock. It was great to work with them and I learned such a lot about their respective cultures. Most notably I learned that whatever our race, we are all just human. We all need love and acceptance, but fear of each other is the biggest obstacle to overcome.

The owners were a long-term gay couple who took me under their wing and became instrumental in shaping my abilities as a young hairdresser. I didn't earn a lot to start with, but the experience and training made up for it. I loved the job and began to attract some amazing clients that even included the President of South Africa. Because the salon was close to the parliament buildings we had a number of politicians and government officers come through, and President F.W. de Klerk was one of them. I was the only one in the shop who was fluent in Afrikaans, the President's first language. It was a real honour to have met the man who led the transitional government and passed the baton on to Mr Nelson Mandela. Those were very exciting times!

Meanwhile, back at the flat things were not so great anymore. Jo had been honest with me about his feelings and claimed to have fallen in love with me, so wanted more than just our friendship. Here I was again, totally unable to commit on that level. One evening we had a big argument about it. We had just spent some time on his parents' farm that he would one day inherit, and his case was that it could all be ours to share. I was tempted, but one thing was missing – I could not be his lover, partner or 'mate' for life. The willingness or attraction was just not there, and I couldn't fake it. He was very much in love with me, but I felt differently.

I hate to admit it but I envied all that he had – his good, caring family and the farm that one day would be his. It made what I perceived I had lost all the more real. If only my parents had made better choices, I too would be set up for life. I was torn. I hated him for having it, but at the same time felt the pull of the possibility of having it all with him. If I could just get myself to say 'yes' to him… but I couldn't. I knew that my intentions would be all wrong.

Our friendship was slowly falling apart.

CHAPTER 12
JULES
+ + +

Not long after this, Jo needed to go home for three or so weeks to help his parents with the harvest. I stayed on in Cape Town, as I had to work.

He had been gone a couple of days when one afternoon after work I dropped by a gay bar around the corner from the salon. I had a couple of drinks, and as I was about to leave, a stranger came to join me at my table. He was from Jo'burg, here on business, and wanted some company. We talked and he bought another round of drinks. After a snack we had more to drink, and to cut a long story short, he ended up coming home with me and we slept together.

The next morning was awkward, as you can imagine. I was slightly hung over, and had a stranger in the flat. He left early and that was it. I could not even remember his name. Just sex, with no breakfast and no strings attached.

Sometime after, Jo returned from his time on the farm, and one of my colleagues invited us to his house for a party at which he had set up a blind date for a friend of his. A whole group of our friends went; we just loved an excuse to drink and hang out. Needless to say, we were all curious to see who the blind date was. On arrival, my colleague opened the door and made it very clear to us that Jules, the blind date organised for him, the guy he had been set up with, was just not compatible; there was no spark between them.

Jules immediately caught my eye, for he was a very handsome man. I can clearly remember turning to my friend Liz and saying, 'I will have him, then!' and I made it my mission to get him. My colleague was just relieved to have someone else interested in Jules, and we just hit it off.

Jules was a fascinating guy, a professional ballet dancer and about ten years older than me. He had left South Africa in the seventies at the height of apartheid, when there was a lot of political unrest following the Sharpeville massacre. He had secured a year's scholarship with the Royal Academy of Dance in London, after which his career took him all over the world with various dance companies.

I was infatuated and so in love with him. He spoke four languages and had been brought up Irish Catholic, but now practised Buddhism. I though his dark curly hair, beautiful green eyes and olive skin were wonderfully exotic. It all happened very quickly and we even entered into a physical relationship straight away. He was very experienced.

Jo saw it coming when we met Jules. They kept it all very composed but the atmosphere was flammable and it was awful to lose a friend that way. Deep down he had hoped that my love would grow towards him. I wasn't proud of how it all happened, but things just couldn't stay the same anymore. So I moved out.

We moved into Jules' sister's house in the City Bowl, Tamboerskloof to be precise. It was only temporary until we could get a flat together, but we happily took the large front room, which had a lovely big enclosed terrace where Jules set up a shrine for Buddha. We smoked a lot a weed. I had to, to get myself to go there, to have sex with him, my new boyfriend and lover.

A couple of months into our relationship, Jules and I were sat together on the sofa, all loved-up. We were watching a documentary on television about living with HIV/AIDS. As you'd expect, we were very interested in this topic as many of our friends had contracted HIV and some had even died from AIDS. This was around the time when HIV/AIDS had really come to the forefront and largely stigmatised the gay community in the world. Cape Town was the gay capital of South Africa and news about HIV/AIDS was all too common. Like everyone, we didn't really believe it would ever happen to us, but due to the promiscuity that sometimes accompanied our lifestyle, we were always at risk.

Then suddenly I got the shock of my life. There we were, all snuggled up on the sofa watching the documentary, when suddenly they were interviewing 'him'! The guy from the gay bar, the one-night stand, the one with no name. He had been living with HIV for eight years – and I had slept with him unprotected. I just froze. I watched as my entire life flashed before me in one single moment. I couldn't move, I couldn't look at Jules; I didn't want to, I was too scared to, too scared to even let him know. 'Oh no! Am I positive? And have I infected Jules as well?' My mind was imploding and my hands became drenched in perspiration.

I had to excuse myself. I felt lightheaded and made my way to the bathroom, where I was sick, sick with shock. I washed my face, like a good boy, slapped my now pale cheeks, and walked out with a smile. Jules had no idea; I played it so cool and carried on as if nothing was wrong.

But inwardly I was in turmoil. What had I done? I was only twenty-three years old, too young to die. Yet I may have not only killed myself but the one I now loved. How stupid of me, how irresponsible.

I decided not to tell Jules; at least, not until I knew for sure. I made a decision to hide this wretched secret from him. I felt so guilty, but I was too scared to share it with him. I could not bear the pain of losing him. I loved him too much.

What followed was the longest six months of my life. That's how long it took to get tested for traces of HIV. I went to work as normal every day, but secretly once a month I visited the clinic without anyone knowing. It was the loneliest I have ever felt. I had to give blood regularly and then wait and wait for the results. Meanwhile, the clinic counselled me to the best of their ability in preparation for the worst outcome.

The fear and anxiety took its toll on me. I kept up the pretence but I was slowly wasting away. At almost six feet tall I now weighed under ten stone; all the signs were there, but I kept a brave face. Everyone else thought that Jules kept me so well. We had moved out from his sister's and were living together in our new flat. You can never be too skinny when you are gay and a stylist. There we were, outwardly enjoying our new and happy life together while I was inwardly wasting away. How ironic.

I started to question life itself. I wondered what the reason for my existence was. What on earth was I here for? Was this all my life was going to be about? In my desperation I quietly cried out to a God that I somehow knew existed but didn't know. 'Please God, heal me! Save me from this!' I bargained with a God I didn't even know or understand for my very life.

The days dragged by and finally, six months later I got the results. No words can describe the relief I felt when I was given the all-clear. But I could not share my miraculous news with anyone, for no one knew. I walked home from the clinic that evening through the Dutch Gardens in the centre of Cape Town, crying my eyes out in relief. I was so lonely. I had no one to share the relief with, the release of having this burden lifted. The faceless ones at the medical clinic knew, but they were strangers.

No one I loved knew or could know. I experienced the depths of loneliness that you can still feel while being in a supposedly loving relationship. It is horrendous.

I reasoned that if I told Jules now, after being together for eight months, things could be over between us. I had risked both our lives by my reckless living. So there it remained, a hidden secret. Jules wasn't in when I got back. He had been working for the National Theatre in Cape Town, rehearsing for *Hair*, the musical. So I phoned a good friend and asked him to come over and we got stoned together. He didn't know about my ordeal either. My celebration was in solitude. It's such a terrible thing to be lonely amongst friends.

CHAPTER 13
CHANGING TIMES
+ + +

With the HIV scare now behind me, life went on and we settled into a routine of doing life as a couple.

We had so much fun in the days that followed my scare; it was as if I had a new lease of life. We frequented the great Cape Town beaches, went clubbing and hung out with friends at every opportunity. I even participated in my first Gay Pride march. This landed my photo on the front page of a major newspaper, which I had not realised until my sister phoned to ask me whether all of this was true. It seems the family had never spoken about any of this to her. I found that sad, but at least it was all out in the open now.

Jules' career was doing well. *Hair*, the musical, was a massive success for him, and I got to help out by giving a salon-sponsored service to the leading star, who was a good friend of ours at the time. He had to be platinum blond for the duration of the show. Parties followed each success, and especially after the final performance at a weekend, when we would be high as kites on amphetamines and ecstasy at the local rave parties in the city.

After *Hair* came *The Boyfriend*, and then *Jesus Christ Superstar*. Our world was full, burning the candle at both ends. The harder we worked, the harder we partied, especially on Sundays when we would crash at someone's house or some pool party. Sometimes we even hit Sandy Bay, the local nudist beach. I was always freaked out by my own nudity but didn't mind others being nude.

Everything came to a halt after *Jesus Christ Superstar*, which coincided with the release of Nelson Mandela in February 1990. His position as deputy president caused the political climate to change drastically in South Africa, and suddenly the previously underprivileged 88 per cent of the black and 'other' population now found itself in an equal position with the white privileged 12 per cent for job opportunities. That meant work dried up for Jules and many other white nationals as new equal opportunity laws were passed. The country was in turmoil.

Sadly the situation at the salon was also changing. My boss was nearing retirement and wanted to go back to the Netherlands. I couldn't blame him for wanting to leave South Africa because there was so much unrest in the country and in the city. Crowds sometimes congregated in the city centre and would suddenly storm down a street smashing all the display-front windows. On several occasions we had to quickly pull down our blackout blinds as we heard the roar of the approaching masses. We turned off the lights and hid our clients in a back storeroom while the window was being smashed at the front. It was a terrifying experience. Understandably, many people fled Cape Town and other major cities, especially those who had money.

One evening, my friend Elise and I went to watch a movie. It was a lovely warm summer's evening so we decided to walk back home. When we were about halfway there, we passed a group of five black youngsters. We had crossed the street to walk on the opposite side because we felt a bit uneasy. The next moment they were right behind us, catching us completely off guard. One drew a knife and held it to my neck. They separated us and I was overcome with fear for Elise. Three of them pushed me down a dark alleyway while the other two stayed with her. They emptied out my wallet, took my watch and a ring I was wearing. Then they demanded I go with them to an ATM to clean out my bank account. I refused and said they would have to kill me. I suppose I could have tried to escape, but I was worried about them hurting Elise so I just stood there, refusing to move. It felt like hours.

When they eventually decided to walk me back up the alleyway, we found her on the street and one of them with his pants down, exposed. He had violated her. Then they just ran off.

We were absolutely hysterical. I cried, apologising for not being man enough to help her. She was reduced to a heap, sobbing and spitting as she was trying to rid herself of what was left of him. It was awful. We carried on walking home, stopped in a park on the way, got completely stoned, arrived home and passed out. We never spoke about it again. I did try, but she didn't want to go there. The fact is, we both knew that going to the authorities would have been a waste of time. This was the new South Africa and the majority of the once-deprived people were still angry and taking it out on random whites. Those were terrible days of transition.

So, with my job up in the air and Jules struggling to even find work, a new opportunity presented itself to us. One of my colleagues was moving to a salon in Somerset West and I was offered the opportunity to go with him. It was too good a chance to miss, so after four years in Cape Town, Jules and I said a sad goodbye to the city.

Somerset West was a very affluent town so Jules was hoping to go into private teaching, as most of the jobs with the National Theatre had dried up. I settled well into the new salon, but things didn't turn out so well for Jules. It seemed everyone was cutting back and there were few opportunities for private tutoring, even from a professional with his wide experience. This depressed him and he wasted his days getting stoned, which put our relationship under a lot of pressure. Financially, we were barely making it on my salary, and to make things worse, the neighbours frowned upon us because we were gay. Even with all the changes taking place in South Africa, the majority of the community were still very conservative and religious.

Things got tougher and tougher for us, and I realised we were approaching rock bottom when we seriously considered an offer to make an adult movie for the porn industry. The money was tempting but I was unable to go there. Strange how the adult movie industry hit on those who had fallen onto hard times. Easy prey, I suppose. That's how desperate it was getting.

In the middle of that challenging time, I received a phone call from Chris, my old college housemate, with some better news. Namibia had just become an independent country, and as part of the celebrations the Miss Universe Beauty Pageant was to be held in the capital, Windhoek, where he worked. They were short of stylists, and the pageant organisers were looking for hair and make-up teams to work on the production of this prestigious event. He wondered if I was interested in joining the team.

Wow! What an opportunity for me and my career. This could change everything. So I excitedly said 'yes' and started making travel plans.

CHAPTER 14
MISS UNIVERSE
+ + +

This Namibian adventure felt like a breath of fresh air after all my recent trials.

I was to stay with Chris' parents, and he lived in a small annex adjoining their house. Jules and I were in agreement about me going, but I knew deep down he was disappointed that we would be apart for a few weeks. I felt guilty leaving him alone and in such a dark place, and swallowed back the tears with great difficulty as I said goodbye to him at Cape Town International Airport.

I arrived at Windhoek and had a night to settle in at the house with Chris and his parents. The next day we drove out to the newly built country club, casino and golf estate, which was being hurriedly finished for the event. To be honest, it was all still a bit of a building site.

We were shown the ropes and allocated a big room situated just to the right of the stage in the great conference hall, where I met the team. There were about sixteen of us stylists, mostly from Namibia. I was so excited; this was going to be an amazing experience!

We soon got to meet the girls from the 130 participating countries. They each came with a chaperone and brought with them a portfolio to show us more or less what they needed for the different scene changes. The hair was to be kept more down for swimwear and more *avant-garde* for evening wear. So we planned everything and then had a run-through of the show. It was riddled with hitches. Many of the girls were suffering with high-altitude sickness and the very dry winter climate played havoc with their hair and delicate skin. So we had some drama to navigate!

The big night arrived. Wow, what a hoot! We worked hard to get them all ready. The room was filled with the smell of hair and beauty products. We were 'high' on hairspray, I think, but it helped to keep the smile on our faces! Miss USA, Chelsea Smith, was crowned Miss Universe and we breathed a satisfied sigh of relief. It was over too soon for me; I'd loved every minute of it.

The rest of my time in Windhoek was wonderful. I had been once before for a holiday when I was six years old, just before my little sister was born. But that was eighteen years ago. We visited a game lodge near the city and I was given a taste of the nightlife. We even ended up at a gay party held in the middle of nowhere because Namibia was very conservative and no gay clubs were officially tolerated at the time, so they rented private venues. I was 'fresh meat' for there were not many gays in this new country of just 1.8 million people. I enjoyed the attention, but was still very much in love with Jules. One of the guys I met there wrote me a letter declaring his fondness. How sweet, I thought, and kept the letter to show Jules later.

Chris and I also did some research. It became apparent to us that there was a gap in the market and that it would be a good idea to open a salon in the capital off the back of the Miss Universe event. We had spoken about one day opening a salon together while we were still students, and this seemed like the perfect opportunity to realise that dream.

My time in Namibia was wonderful. There was something

indescribably energising about spending time somewhere new, especially in a desert country. The aridness, the desolation, the emptiness; it stirred something in my heart which I could not really describe at the time. It left me wondering what life was all about once again. What about Jules? I thought. I'd been away from him for ten days and coped better than I had expected to. I missed him, but there was something quite exciting about being away. Was it the freedom of not having the responsibility of a relationship? Or was it just that I enjoyed being on holiday alone? It's strange how, when you're away from what's familiar, you end up questioning things. And there was plenty of room to think in the Namib Desert.

When the time came for me to leave, I couldn't contain my emotions. I cried so much saying goodbye to Chris and his parents; I just couldn't believe it was all over. I didn't get paid at all for this event, but I did have a certificate from Donald Trump's Miss Universe Association for services rendered, and I'd had an awesome experience. You couldn't put a price on the wonderful time I'd had. So I left Namibia with a heavy heart.

On returning home, I found that things had changed. While I'd been away Jules had convinced himself that I'd had an affair. He didn't understand how I could have returned from working at this event without earning any money. Neither did it help when he discovered the letter from my admirer in my wallet; it just convinced him even more that I had cheated on him. The more I tried to explain, the less it helped the situation. To top it off, I decided to share with him how much I had enjoyed my time away and that I was somehow moved and deeply touched by my time in the desert. There was something mysterious about experiencing the solitude. The vastness of the empty expanse caused me to question the very meaning of life and my somehow small existence.

It took just one innocent remark from me. I wanted to know what he thought, so I asked him, 'What do you think God thinks about this, about us?' Not that I knew the answer to this profound question, and I can't even remember why I had brought God into the conversation in the first place. But it did not help. He was hurt, angry and jealous of the life I had been leading without him, and his suspicions about my 'affair' only deepened.

All of a sudden, we were over; our almost three-year relationship was finished. Just like that; no real fighting, no arguments, it just fizzled out. Could it really have been that easy? Is love not worth fighting for? Was this love at all? I moved into the spare bedroom.

Jules packed up his belongings while I was at work. It was painful to see the pile of boxes grow each day and the interior of the house change. Then one night I came back from work and he was gone. He even took our cat! I can't remember whether I cried more about the cat or about him. It was just more loss. I didn't even know where he had gone.

His going left me stressed out. I had the duplex apartment lease to sort out and all the things that went with it, as well as suddenly having to cope with living alone again. Here I was in one of the most exciting career seasons of my life, but my personal life was in a mess again.

Off the back of Miss Universe, I had done a press interview that had greatly benefitted the salon where I was working. My soon-to-be sister-in-law had posed with me for a photo for the article and it had brought in many more clients. So work was growing and exciting, but my home and personal life was a shambles. I drank heavily to cover the pain and partied as much as I could to avoid the reality of my situation.

During this period, my younger brother got married. I couldn't face going to the wedding by myself so I had to phone an old mutual friend and managed to get back in touch with Jules and asked him to come with me, which he did. This brought some sense of comfort, but it was a little awkward. My ma and *Ouma* came for their hair styling before the wedding, and then the four of us all went together. They tolerated us and all we did; the drugs, the drinking and the lifestyle. Somehow they just kept loving us, never confronting us or challenging it in any way.

Soon after the wedding, it all came to a head. I had lost so much weight that friends and colleagues were getting concerned. Doing a lot of weed and the heavy drinking were wrecking me. I couldn't remember being more unhappy in my life.

One weekend when I was free, Ma came to pick me up and took me to *Ouma's*. I cried the whole way. I cried about Jules, the cat we had that he took, and the hopelessness of my current situation. My evenings were lonely, I hardly had any furniture after the spilt and very little food to eat, as every penny was being consumed by running my life of addiction. Paying to stay on in the duplex with all its expenses seemed an impossible task. Killing myself seemed like a great idea again, but I didn't have the guts to do it. I didn't really want to end my life now, but something had to change.

I spoke with *Ouma* and she thought it would be a good idea to get the local *dominee* (reverend) from the Dutch Reformed Church to come and visit me. I was willing to try anything, so arranged for him to come. His visit was awkward because we didn't have much to say to each other, and he seemed a bit lost on how to help. I was embarrassed to have him in my now very empty duplex and I did not know where to start. So it came and went, a non-event.

From time to time I did pick up my Bible. Yes, I had a few, but this one I got when I was confirmed in the Dutch Reformed Church. Reading it would just make me feel condemned and scared. I mean, the Bible is the Word of God! Did he even like me? Never mind love me?

It had to end. I had to draw a line and break this spiral of mounting poverty and despair. So, I decided to take my friend Chris up on his offer from a few months before. I gave him a call and, just like that, I was going to Windhoek to set up a salon with him. I was going to leave all this and start again.

I gave my notice at the salon in Somerset West, which didn't go down well given the recent increase in clients. But I had to go.

CHAPTER 15
NEW LIFE
+ + +

I was twenty-four and on my way to set up my own salon with Chris, in a new city in a new country with a new culture. A new life beckoned. Was I crazy or just brave?

Saying goodbye to my ma was the hardest thing I had to do. We both somehow knew this was probably the last time I would be living in South Africa which made it all the more poignant.

When I got there, everything was all lined up. We moved into the annex of Chris' parents' property while setting up the business. The shop was one we had been to see when I was there for Miss Universe a few months earlier. It was part of a lovely garden centre, something of a concept store more than a standard unit. There was a Jacuzzi shop, an art gallery, a frame shop, landscapers, bistro, silk flower shop, a beautician and even a jeweller in there with us.

A full refit was needed before we could open, which introduced me to lots more friends from the Windhoek gay community, as it seemed many of them had the skills to help us. We needed shopfitters, interior designers, tradesmen, an accountant, a banker – pretty much everything. The gay community may have been small, but it was certainly very well-connected.

Behind the scenes, the mammoth process of getting me a visa so I could stay in the country and work had started. The new Namibian government was trying to employ locals as a priority, unless you could show you had a skill that nobody else had. It did make sense, but meant I had a long battle to make my particular case. I won in the end, but the salon had been open a long while by the time it was all finalised, so it was all a bit scary.

The refit work went on at a pace. Before long, the shopfitters were installing the worktops alongside a local artist who was crafting marble-effect *trompe l'oeil* on the walls. The ceiling was draped in metres of *voile*. In short, we created a neo-classic contemporary garden room. It had lovely big windows that overlooked the plants in the garden centre, which in an arid desert country was a luxurious bonus. It looked amazing.

It was a huge job to get it all done as close to the end of the Miss Universe pageant as possible. But we did it and managed to make the connection that the amazing people who had done the hair for the pageant were about to open in the city. 'Co-Hairance' had come to the city. We were buzzing; two guys in their twenties about to take the world by storm!

The shop took off with a bang. The word about us travelled like wildfire and the diary was filled in no time. We definitely had a good thing going. Not only were we good at what we did, we were gay and proud and everyone wanted to come and have a look. We served our clients a variety of free alcoholic drinks as part of the experience, which suited the local culture very well. That community really knew how to party, and many a night we had to order taxis to return our clients home safely.

The months passed and we partied as hard as we worked. We were young and able to keep it up, so our fan club grew. It felt awesome to be admired for what we did in the salon, but my heart still ached for love; I was lonely and still feeling the loss of my stable relationship with Jules. So I soon started sleeping around. It was the only way I knew how to fill the emptiness in my heart. But then I reasoned to myself that it was probably easier to have no commitments; relationships are hard and challenging, especially if you feel inadequate to maintain them. And I needed to prioritise running the salon; I had staff, a business partner, clients and responsibility. So the search for a stable relationship was put on the back-burner and compensated for by one-night stands.

Meanwhile, we made lots of money, which became a strong motivation for me at the time. Money, fame and being one of the best salons in the city all drove me on, and helped fill my inner heartache. Around that time we won the tender to do the hair and styling for a major news anchor with the Namibian Broadcasting Corporation; she was a well-known personality. In exchange we got national publicity at the end of the eight o'clock news. It was fantastic publicity and created a lot of attention for us, so we just kept growing.

Chris and I did have a bit of strife between us at one point, all centred around me being the one who had all the 'big city experience' of working in Cape Town. So we resolved it by bringing in a third (silent) partner who would mediate when we could not agree on things. But overall, we were flying!

Much to my delight, Ma and *Ouma* came to visit me, and we had a fantastic time. We went sightseeing and I put them up in a beautiful five-star resort on the coast. Unbeknown to them, the stay was a prize that I had won at a drag competition hosted by the same country club and casino where the Miss Universe pageant had been held. I was really messed up when it came to my sexual identity, and being a drag queen somehow fed the search. I was even seriously considering a sex change at that time; anything to make me get loved more.

During my spare time I explored the country and its beauty

captivated me. To the north it is lush and green and extends to the spectacular Victoria Falls, while to the south there are dry savannah plains that are full of fossils with a strange beauty all of their own. Along the west coast, the Namib Desert flows into endless beaches including the well-known Skeleton Coast, where literally thousands of shipwrecks lie exposed. To the east is the Kalahari Desert with its game reserves and settlements of bushmen. The country is rich in natural resources, its wildlife and national parks making it a feast for any nature-lover. I also loved the fusion of cultures I encountered in Namibia; something like thirteen different people-groups coexist and integrate across its scattered population of only 2 million people. As you can tell, I loved everything about it.

Namibia's cultural diversity was also reflected in my clients; they were a characterful bunch. I had some who owned private game reserves, and we had many a lion cub in the salon while being hand-raised; this was not your average salon! Many of them celebrated our 'gayness', but others really struggled with our lifestyle, particularly those with Christian beliefs or backgrounds. I remember looking up from my client's hair one day to see a man laying his hands on our massive shop window and praying 'in tongues' to drive the demons out of us. I was livid and practically foaming at the mouth about his sticky fingerprints all over the freshly cleaned windows, which probably didn't help his perception of me!

This was a very good new life. Materially I was making a lot of money, and I'd lots of friends and action in my life. I looked the part, but the truth was that I still ached on the inside; I was a lost soul, trying to find myself, and the true meaning of my life.

CHAPTER 16
PEACE
+ + +

Not all my Christian clients tried to cast demons out of the salon! Others were kinder to me, especially one man, Eddy. He was a Christian with a different attitude all together.

Eddy had a good job in the city, had been Namibia's national badminton champion and had also been a model at one time. I thought he was very handsome. Eddy was also a very gentle-hearted and sincere Christian who I soon discovered was also a leader at his local church. He once told me he was the worship pastor – whatever that was. He had no shame in sharing his love for God, like some of my other religious clients, but he was somehow not like the rest; he never judged me. To tell you the truth, he did not once refer to my sexuality or lifestyle. He was just different.

He had been my client for many months and over time we became close. I really fancied him; well, I thought I did. There was just something really attractive about him that I couldn't fully put my finger on. We became friends, and he would sometimes come to the shop after work just to hang out and end up helping somehow. There was always something to do, like towels to be thrown in the wash, products to sort, drink orders to take, clients to chat to, and he just pitched in. He was so free, and not freaked out by me, like some of the other Christians I knew.

Our friendship generated quite a lot of gossip. Little wonder, really: there was me, who had slept with most of the guys in the gay community, and Eddy, who was well known as the worship pastor from the local church. What was he doing hanging out with me? Why did my tainted reputation never seem to bother him? Never mind the fact that most suspected us of having a relationship.

Well, I suppose we did have one; a relationship, that is. But not the one I lusted after. He loved me like a friend and shared his life with me. He didn't even mind that my intentions were not always good, because I made it clear that I loved him and wanted to sleep with him. And he kept on being just steady, loving me as a friend. Eddy was the first man who didn't want something from me; he wasn't in my life just to get his 'rocks off' or to join the Ennrich fan club.

I still didn't drive because of the fear I carried from my father's car accident, so Eddy sometimes drove me home when I was not using a taxi. We talked about our respective workdays and he would frequently share about what he believed were God-ordained meetings with people; they seemed like miracles to him, I suppose. It was just a natural part of his life, as was his love for Jesus. Sometimes I found myself staring at him and secretly envying what he had, the way he managed in life – because he had some real challenges but always seemed to cope well and come through stable and smiling; the polar opposite of how I had handled mine.

Deep down I wondered if Eddy's God could ever love someone like me. I mean, he kept telling me that God loved me, but I had had so many bad experiences with God and church as a child that I just could not compute that Eddy's God and the God of my childhood were even the same beings.

As a child, I'd had to listen to Bible reading and prayers with my stepdad, which I hated; not because it was the Bible, but because it was him. Then, Sunday after Sunday I had been dressed up and dragged to a boring church service, sometimes twice a day in temperatures well into forty degrees Celsius. Relief did sometimes come through the self-induced nosebleed I perfected just to avoid going! I had also had the heartache of trying to integrate into a new church after the divorce, and that put me off forever. I recognised the same judgemental God as being the one behind the idiots who shouted me down at Gay Pride while waving their 'turn or burn' placards. He may even have been behind the tongue-speaking exorcist who left his messy fingerprints on my shop window.

Eddy's God was obviously different. He gave him strength and serenity to navigate life in a way which attracted people to him, not put them off. Even gays like me! It got me thinking very deeply. I kept asking myself if it could ever really be true that God could love me. Could it be true that Eddy's God is the source of love in him, for me? I wondered.

It reminded me of the sign above the pulpit in the church I went to as a child that said, 'God is Love'. Did that mean he loved even me? I even remembered the hymn we had sung at my father's funeral, 'What a friend I have in Jesus' when I was just seven years old. Does this Jesus really want to be my friend, I thought, like Eddy is now?

I knew one thing for sure; I was in a mess. No matter how hard I tried or how much I did; no matter how frequently I partied, drank, smoked, slept around or tried to make and keep friends, it was just not enough. What was I missing? Could it be God? Could it be this Jesus?

All this was depressing me. I felt was as if I was sat on the brink of a very deep and dark abyss, with both legs dangling over the edge. I could just slip into its darkness at any point. Not that

I ever admitted to feeling it at the time; it was just my inner angst fuelled by fear, denial and pride.

One evening in May 1996, Eddy had driven me home once again. And like most previous times he had chatted about his day. This time I just listened. He was going on about God and his relationship with Jesus again; how he had received strength and wisdom from the Holy Spirit for the challenges he'd had to face that day. If only I could access some of that strength, I pondered. I was so desperate for something to change in my life.

Eddy had gone through to the kitchen to make us coffee and I was sat on the carpet in the lounge, deep in thought. My heart was pounding and my thoughts were racing as I kept thinking: Does Eddy's God really, really love me? Does he accept me, just as I am? I knew what Eddy would say; I had heard him explain it so many times. It was as if I was gradually getting some understanding, but still had so many questions about this God and what it all meant.

Did I just have to believe it anyway and get my questions answered later? My heart was pounding in my ears by now. I ventured to ask Eddy's God a question for the very first time: 'Jesus, are you real?' And as I asked, a strange warm presence seemed to fill the room. 'Is this presence that I am feeling right now, you?' I asked. My thoughts were racing like a roller coaster out of control, but in my heart I was aware that something or someone was right there. Peace was there like I had never felt before; a peace that seemed to want to invade my inner being. 'Is this him? Is this somehow God with me right now?'

The penny dropped. A light went on in my heart. Yes, it was! Jesus was here in the room with me. He wanted to be a part of my life. It was his love I felt, his intense love for me, and my eyes were now welling up with tears. And the more I dared to believe it was

Jesus who was touching my heart, an immense feeling of awe came over me. I decided there and then to believe him, to put whatever little faith I had in him, not in myself anymore. He felt so close to my heart, like no one had ever felt before. I cried from the depths of my being, 'Please help me, I need you.' I groaned as I called for him, from deep within me.

An indescribable peace flooded my insides. A colossal sigh followed as a weight left my shoulders. Love, his love, flooded my heart as he entered my life. I didn't deserve this, but it was my first taste of God's love freely given to me. I had no words as I sat there with Jesus. It felt like I had finally come home.

The tears were now flowing freely. I wasn't alone anymore. I felt complete and accompanied for the first time in my life. I felt a deep reverence for him, a sort of love and gratefulness all at the same time. I instinctively knew that he knew me, all about me, and still loved me. I felt safe. I somehow knew I was being saved, saved from myself and everything that had haunted me.

Eddy came back from the kitchen with hot drinks, his eyes full of tears now. He knew what was happening, even though I had no words for it. He had no words for me, either, just a hug and the comfort of his friendship.

I met Jesus that night. He had become my friend through the love of my friend Eddy.

I couldn't stop crying as the layers and weight of carrying my own life were gradually peeled back by God's gracious love. I cried about it all: my life, my desperate need for love, my dead father, my struggle to speak to Ma, and my weird relationships with family. I cried about the abuse, my own stupid choices; the drugs and drinking, the sex, all the men in my life. I cried about my fear, loneliness and confusion. It all came tumbling out. I was being emptied of myself and the new Ennrich was being birthed.

From now on I would no longer be alone; it would be 'us', not 'me'. Christ in me, and I in him.

CHAPTER 17
THE NEW MAN
+ + +

Eddy left my life as gently as he had entered it. It amused me to think that God had used a beautiful man to catch my attention in order to reveal his greater love to me. He knew me so well; but then, he knows everything.

In the weeks that followed I met some of the Christians in Eddy's world, including his pastors, a lovely American couple, and I became more and more aware of just how many Christians had been praying for me. Strange, I thought, as they were the very ones that annoyed me so much! But it touched me deeply that God has used these people to pray for my soul; he had entrusted them with my life somehow.

I still had feelings for Eddy that made our friendship increasingly difficult now. The truth is, I fancied him more than was good for me. Then one day I read the story of David and Jonathan in the Bible. They deeply loved each other as friends, but had to separate because of the greater purpose of God, and I felt the same applied to Eddy and me. So we released each other to pursue all we each believed we were yet to become in God. It was tough and scary, but God was in it with us.

I now realise that a new man was born the night I met Jesus, a new man with a God-given purpose to accomplish. So every area of my life now wanted to and had to be submitted to God's perfect will. It was and is a process, and I am not fully there yet, even after all these years. But God is patient and works with us one step at a time as we take simple steps of faith in obedience to his revealed will. And parting company with Eddy was one such step – that's why it was never shrouded with tension or bitterness; it was all part of God's good plan.

This new man now also had to get his head around his homosexuality. I had always known that homosexuality was a sin, for I had read it in the Bible and heard it declared to be so by many condescending Christians over the years. But what I didn't know was that Jesus was the answer to the problem of sin in this world, and my sin in particular, until he revealed it to me. He never called me gay; Jesus never once called me by my sin. Instead, he came to take my sins away by his blood that was shed on the cross. Jesus died for all my sins, so that means he died for homosexuality as well. The old Ennrich had died with Christ, and the new Ennrich had been born that night.

Everything that happened after my 'new birth' was a process of renewal in me, which had to include dealing with the lingering consequences of my sin. The sin of homosexuality had left a big mark on me, and it was now my job to deal with its consequences, with the help of God who was with me. I was slowly being changed in my heart and in my thinking.

Of course, the 'old me' and the 'new me' sometimes came into conflict. But my job was to remember that the old Ennrich was dead and I was to live in the light of that reality. I had resolutely decided to follow Jesus and live his way, and what followed was an amazing time of being saved from myself, and all that I'd carried for the previous twenty-six years. Jesus had truly become my Saviour.

Back at the salon, things were different. My gay friends, the business and the partnership had suddenly lost their common ground. The 'gel' was gone; the 'gel' of camp banter and the whole gay scene ceased to be the glue that held my life together. I didn't quite feel a part of the salon and all that it represented anymore.

It was tough because I couldn't really explain it. As much as I tried, in those early days of my walk with God I felt the change acutely but couldn't describe it in a way that brought understanding to those who observed it. When I did try, the misunderstanding on everyone's faces spoke volumes. They just did not seem to get it, or get me. It's so easy! I thought. All you have to do is believe, and everything else will change; you can have another life. There is another life, parallel to this one – more real than this one. I even used C.S. Lewis' *Narnia Chronicles* to try to explain myself. All you have to do is choose; it's *your* choice to choose Jesus, the new way. Your old way may not have always been your choice, but you can choose to believe Jesus, and he makes a new way.

I suppose my friends were unable to see what I could see, or perhaps they did not *want* to see. I later realised that it took both God's grace and my response of faith to receive Jesus. The sobering experience of having to come to the end of 'yourself' was and is a massive realisation.

It took courage for me to admit that we had all been sincerely wrong about being gay, and that the only truth I found was him. I was a new creation in him, the old had gone and the new had come, as it says in the New Testament (see 2 Corinthians 5:17).

I now needed new relationship 'gel' to hold the various expressions of my life together, and soon realised that people who shared my new-found faith in God were it. That probably meant church, which was not a good thought; I had so many bad memories of church, so found myself in something of a dilemma.

God was so faithful with me in those early days. I kept on

speaking to my clients about my experience, and it was there I met Claudette. She and her husband had been praying for me and they now took me into their lives. I wanted to go back to church, even though I still had so many feelings of rejection around church that I battled with. But the two of them gave me courage to go, and most importantly, someone to sit with.

Words cannot describe the mixture of emotions I felt on that first day in church. It was a lively gathering, and quite a few of the congregation were clients of the salon. But you should have seen some of their faces when they saw me! Some were accepting, but sadly, some were filled with disbelief that someone like me could be 'made new', changed, 'born again'. Still others were content with who they thought I was, and didn't see the need for me to change at all – but I knew I needed to. This broke my heart. I wondered, had they not met Jesus in their once-broken lives and experienced his healing power and love for them?

So, in church I had to start again and go through the whole process of belonging to a new community. I met people from all walks of life, and they shared their life stories from time to time when we met. Their stories just confirmed what I was learning, that I was being called from my old gay life into a new life of surrender to God, which would be led by his Holy Spirit. It inspired me to surrender fully to him and make the choice to live a life of love for God and for others. It was the least I could do for the one who had given his all for me.

Belonging to this new church community was a real practical challenge, because I had no idea about how to belong to anyone or anything. My past references were a dysfunctional family and the gay life. I had so much to learn, and particularly struggled with boundaries. Remember, I used to sleep with men. Now they were to be my brothers. These were crazy new times! I'd also had very little to do with girls, but that too was changing as I did life with Jesus and his family, the church. And slowly, I began to change.

Things started to make more sense as I did everyday life with God. I started speaking to him non-stop; I was in a constant conversation with God in my head and heart as I did life – I now know that is what the Bible calls praying without ceasing (see 1 Thessalonians 5:17). I started reading the Bible, too, hanging out with others in the church world and asking God daily to fill me with his Holy Spirit.

There was so much to learn. My habits, my thoughts, the way I spoke, the way I did things and the things I used to do, all had to change. Yet it was painfully slow sometimes. Why was that? I wondered. Even though I became well-integrated into the church community and was serving in a number of areas of church life, why did I have to work so hard on the change process? Couldn't God have just changed me in an instant? I came to realise that the way God works is in a partnership with us; he doesn't treat us like puppets. We choose to live each day with him, and those free choices are what lead to lasting change. The Christian life is relational from start to finish.

Another thing I wrestled with was the reason for my past. Why, I pondered, did I have to experience my old life with its suffering, loss and pain? Why did I have to go through it? Was there anything good that could come from it? And how did I get past all the hurt in my soul, and the memories? My heart was heavy and I started to grieve about all my past hurts. But for the first time, I grieved with God at my side. Crying before God was amazing as he washed away the lingering guilt, shame and brokenness, and healed my broken heart. I experienced the reality of what Jesus came to do:

He has sent me to bind up the broken-hearted, to proclaim freedom for the captives ... and provide for those who grieve in Zion – to bestow on them a crown of beauty instead of ashes, the oil of joy instead of mourning, and a garment of praise instead of a spirit of despair. (Isaiah 61:1–3)

It was, and still is, a choice to give my feelings of hurt and bad memories to him. But in that walking, talking and sharing, I found forgiveness for myself and that I could forgive those who had abused and hurt me.

I had to forgive my dad for leaving us and for dying. I had to forgive my messed-up family and those who had abused me. I had to forgive myself for my bad choices – the drugs and sex and alcohol. Again and again God gave me the opportunity to give it to him and leave it there, to nail it to the cross where he had made the ultimate sacrifice for my sin. It was so powerful, this incredible truth that he had forgiven all my hurt, brokenness and all my sins.

The weight of it all just kept on falling off my chest. I had never felt so light in all my life; so peaceful. Thank you, Jesus!

As time went on, I increasingly knew I had to find a way out of the business. The salon confronted me with my old life in an unhelpful way and was clearly not part of my new future. It didn't help that all my new Christian clients and friends came to the shop where we openly discussed the goodness of God. It caused so much friction, as light and darkness don't mix, but how do you keep quiet about this good news?

So one Saturday evening I decided to tell Chris that I wanted out. At first he was quite amicable, but within a few days things changed and he made it very difficult for me. Being a partner in the salon where drugs were freely available left me in a compromised position. Maybe it was anger or fear on his part, I just don't know. There was a risk of my deportation if the authorities caught up with all the drug abuse in and around the salon. I had to move on, and we went to the lawyers to have our agreement dissolved. It was messy, to say the least. Dissolving a partnership is like going through divorce; it's pretty awful. But it had to be done, and was done.

That left me as a South African citizen in a foreign country, and under the terms of my visa, I could not work for anyone else but only run my own business. So, much prayer went into what my next step should be, and God answered me!

I had a client friend, an affluent German farmer who was a distant relative of Chris, my former business partner. This guy and his family had been ever so kind to me over the years. One day he approached me and made me an offer I just could not believe.

'How would you like some money to set up your own business?' he asked. 'What, really?' I said, while thinking, could this be the answer to my prayers? Well, that was it! Amazing. It taught me that God was not only my Saviour and healer, but was also my provider. He works in mysterious ways – even through a rich German farmer!

What a break that was. The transition between shops took a couple of months, which meant I was broke, but God was so faithful in looking after me. Church friends and clients dropped in from time to time with meals and to encourage me. Erna, a very special lady, took me under her wing. She owned the local beauty suppliers in the city and took me on her rounds to meet all the salon owners. I got to meet them all, and on top of that she fed me every lunchtime for months. What kindness.

I took some of our staff with me to the new shop. Meanwhile,

Chris, my former partner, decided to take a complete break from doing life in Namibia and went to work on cruise ships. The break from my old business life was complete.

Business was good. I had a tremendous amount of support, and many clients followed me to the new shop. Honestly, though, I had no desire to grow this business, nor did I have the greatest business skills. But I had to earn some money to pay the bills while a far greater dream was incubating in my heart; a dream I was desperately excited to pursue in due time.

On the relationship front, I was still lonely, yet not alone anymore. I knew I wanted a mate in life and that God was not calling me to a life of singleness, but it did not eat away at me like it had done before I met Jesus. Instead, I was trusting God for the right person at the right time.

One day I spotted something in the Bible that inspired me. I was a new man, a 'new Adam', you might say, and this 'new Adam' was looking for his mate, much like the original Adam had done in the biblical accounts. When Adam became lonely, God made Eve from one of his ribs to be his helper, partner and wife. Each was created by God to complement the other: one male, one female. Thus, the first marriage took place and they became 'one flesh' before God (Genesis 1–3). This was God's ideal; his original intention for marriage, and that is what I knew I must aspire to.

This understanding motivated and inspired this new man to dare to start trusting God for his Eve too.

CHAPTER 18
RETHINKING GIRLS
+ + +

François was a close friend, a real brother to me. We had met through church, and found a real freedom to share our hopes and dreams with each other. He knew that I wanted a soulmate in life, my Eve. However, I was approaching thirty by now and considered virtually 'on the shelf' by the popular culture I lived and worked in. So we talked and prayed about it together regularly.

I used to make a little list of what I wanted in a wife. She first had to love Jesus like I did. Then, being in the beauty industry, she also had to be beautiful – a bit shallow I know, but I wanted someone who made my heart race when I saw her. She must be intelligent, and funny, and a bit cheeky – I didn't want some bland, characterless soul, even if she was a stunner. And so the list grew as I got to know myself a little better.

François would laugh with me about it, and then pray. He was such a good friend. Eventually, I came to the conclusion that all I wanted was a great friendship with her. I just wanted someone who was willing to partner with me in life, someone I could love unconditionally and who would love me back that way.

As time passed, I got impatient with God, sometimes even doubting that anyone would have me at all, given my past. François, who was also single, would say to me, 'Ennrich, stop being so dramatic! Enough of the dress rehearsals. Be patient!'

We were both serving actively in the local church and there

was no shortage of girls, it has to be said. Some of them became quite close friends, but I had not been on a date with girl for a very long time, since the time in high school, and I was pretty intimidated by the process. I had no idea how to approach it so made lots of clumsy mistakes. After all, in a normal family a young man learns primarily from his father and mother about how to interact with and treat the opposite sex. It felt like I had lost out on that positive exposure; I knew how to do it badly, but that didn't mean I could just do the opposite and it would work.

The process also raised lots of questions for me about what a true man of God actually looks like. What is his gender? And what was I, given my past? Was I bi, gay or straight? Something inside me rebelled against believing I was completely straight, because so much of the hurt and disappointment in my past, and in the world as we know it, came through so-called straight men, and I didn't want to be like them.

More broadly, I had many questions about God-centred gender and sexuality. What exactly does this new person, this new man or new creation look like? I was scared, as my examples of gender, sexuality and intimacy were mostly from my past experiences. So how was I to engage in all of this as a new creation? I had to start reading up in God's Word to find out what he said about it. Thankfully I discovered there were many examples that could shape my thinking, and my relationships at church also proved valuable for wisdom as I explored the Scriptures.

In the Bible I found men like David who, like me, had fallen into sexual immorality. It had huge consequences for him and the lady involved, resulting in them losing a child together and David's reign being troubled for many years thereafter. But regardless of his sin, God, in his infinite grace, forgave and restored him fully when he repented. David still had to live with the consequences of his sin, but before God, he was in peace and fully reconciled. God still regarded him as being 'a man after his own heart' (1 Samuel 13:14) and I identified with that. That was the type of man I wanted to be. I didn't want to be straight, gay, bi or whatever; I wanted to be a man after God's own heart.

My next big question was very practical: 'How do you even start liking a girl?' Come on, now, you know what I mean; this was all new to me. Boys learn a lot about girls from their mothers. They learn to appreciate nurture, softness, protection and security, both physical and emotional. But my experience with Ma was tough, cold, distant, hard work, and I struggled to trust her. Years in the salon had taught me how to 'maintain' a girl, but it was all very superficial and of little use to me in this current quest.

Once again I found so much comfort in the story of David, whose parents did not even bother to acknowledge he existed when the prophet Samuel came to anoint one of their sons to be the next future king of Israel (1 Samuel 16). How could his parents just not be bothered to have all their sons in line when Samuel, a major prophet, called around to anoint one of their boys to be the next future king of Israel? This must have hurt David, and he voices his complaint to the Lord in the Psalms of how he had been deserted by his mother and father (Psalm 27:10). He found restoration by calling out to God, and I had to do the same.

One big thing I have learned is that God parents me better than my human ones. He knows where we are broken and wants to make us whole again. All we have to do is to be honest with him and patiently surrender to his care. That's what David did, and he later sings God's praises. God, being Spirit, has all the attributes of both parents; therefore he can and wants to gather us like a mother. God gathers people as a group, but he also 'gathers' each individual when we receive Jesus Christ (see Luke 13:34). How awesome is God's love for me that he wants to gather all the loose bits in me and put them back in their rightful place.

Another good friend of mine, Dirk, a *dominee* in the Dutch Reformed Church, gave me this piece of advice and wisdom regarding girls: 'A little bit, often,' he said. He explained that this is the way to introduce change, to have initial exposure in small quantities, and as often as I would dare to confront my own fears. I say 'fears' deliberately because the fact was, I was afraid of them – yes, of girls! But why was I afraid of them? I did a bit of soul-searching and came to the conclusion that I just did not know or trust them, and now was the time to face my fears – my fear of girls – the fear that was stuck to my emotions linked to my past. I needed to rethink girls, this time with God, allowing him to restore me as I released those emotions and memories to him.

Samantha came into my life when I least expected it. Good mutual friends of ours, James and Roelene, were to be married in the September of 2002. I had met Samantha five months earlier, at a health food party. It was a rather formal introduction. She had just been for a swim and neither of us was really in the mood for small talk with a stranger. But when I saw her I thought, wow, she is a beautiful girl; tall, blue eyes, and thick, titian hair. She impressed me, but I never thought anything would come of it.

Unbeknown to me, on several occasions Roelene had tried to get Samantha and I together without any success – the little matchmaker! After that first meet, the months flew past and soon their big day arrived.

It was the morning of their wedding. Samantha was Roelene's maid of honour, and I had been asked to do the bride's hair. Samantha had an appointment at another salon for some reason, but she soon returned to join the bride as we prepared. We were all so excited for James and Roelene. They both served the Lord, having met through church, and today they were getting married. It gave me hope.

I was just about to finish Roelene's make-up when she asked me whether I would mind doing Samantha's make-up as well. Since I was not running late – a minor miracle in itself – I agreed to do it. Was this a set-up, or what? The bride left us to get on with her big day, and there I was, alone with Samantha in the chair, and as close as you get when you do someone's make-up. Yes, this was a set-up!

We talked. Samantha already knew about me through her parents, because I had been in the same church as them for a period after I was first saved, and they had shared my story with her. Samantha grew up in Windhoek, Namibia, in a normal home, by my standards. Her parents were still married after thirty or so years and she had a sister eighteen months older than her. One of her own family members, who she was and is very close to and loved dearly, was in the fashion industry and lived a gay lifestyle, similar to my own. He lived at home with them so she had been exposed to his lifestyle at close quarters. I also discovered that during her years at university there was further exposure through various friends who came out as gay. Was God preparing her for something? I couldn't help wondering. I even dared to ask myself, 'Was she prepared just for me?'

We got on very well; it felt like we were in a bubble that existed outside of time and space. This was fun and she was not all that scary, I thought. We talked and talked. I shared a little about my past, and how I got to this point in life. She listened. It was so good to talk to someone who really listened.

She had made a commitment to Jesus when she was younger,

but after leaving school to study medicine in South Africa at the Stellenbosch University, she bumped into a vibrant student church family where she recommitted her life to God at the age of eighteen.

Samantha had the privilege of studying with the support of her parents and the Namibian government who, through the Ministry of Education and Culture, supplied her with a bursary to complete medicine, on the basis that she had to sign a contract and commit to working her years back with the Namibian government following her graduation.

She had grown in her faith and walk with God, trusting in him, and in short had no desire to 'mess about' with dating, thus running the risk of having her heart broken, or even worse, causing someone else hardship. She trusted God for a husband to 'pursue her in marriage'. This had always been the desire and the prayer of her heart, and she trusted him for it.

Funny, yet amazing to think that she had spent six years doing medicine and another three years working, holding onto God's promises and with this desire in her heart! And here she was, in my chair, in my salon, with me doing her make-up!

I shared a little about how I met Jesus, and what God had been doing in my life in the last five years, and that I was not in a particularly good place at this point in time. But more about this shortly.

We got on. Wow! Actually, we got on really well.

Off we went to the wedding, followed by a reception at a beautiful game lodge, not too far from the city. It was spectacular! James and Roelene, the handsome couple, thought it would be a good idea to seat all their single friends at one extra-large table, just so they could mingle. Ha! Clever, I thought. So I sneaked into the reception venue beforehand to change the seating arrangement so I could sit next to Samantha.

There were complications, some unbeknown to me; Samantha had her eye on the single guy she was supposed to be sitting next to. He was a pilot. However, he was delayed due to work commitments and arrived late, so thankfully I had a window of opportunity in which to impress this girl. This was my moment!

We talked and talked, then danced till late in the evening. It was so much fun. Girls are fun, you know! But we were not alone at the wedding. I was not alone with her now, sat at the table at the reception.

CHAPTER 19
COMPROMISE
+ + +

I must pause with you here for an honesty moment. Remember, I had told Samantha I wasn't in a particularly good place at that point, which was a bit of an understatement. Let me explain this complexity.

About four years into my walk with God, I nearly gave it all up. I was struggling with relationships at church and had become very disillusioned with things. It was just after a very dear friendship with a girl at church had gone completely wrong because of my inability to understand women and be patient. Talk about throwing an adult tantrum! I fell into major discontentment with everything relating to God and the church, and slowly started steering back towards the only other life I knew. That included noticing guys again, as I actively went looking for their company. I was angry with God and felt that I had 'given it all up' for him, and why? Just to be alone with no mate in life? I had lost my trust in him. Looking back now, I realise I should have taken my complaint to him and reasoned with him like Job, a great hero of faith in the Bible, did. But I didn't, I left church instead; well that's not quite true either, I was asked to leave. It was a mess. The close girl friend I mentioned before was the daughter of one of the church leaders and she had fallen in love with me, but I didn't feel the same way about her and was thoroughly confused by it all. Her ma had got involved and asked me to 'release her', but I wasn't holding her! So let's just say I was not in the best of places when I left.

The journey from my once-gay lifestyle meant that I frequently got opportunities in churches, and even some schools, to tell the story of how I met Jesus. These opportunities increased after I attended a pro-gay meeting at the University of Namibia – I'd gone in the hope of bringing the message of Christ our Saviour to those present. And this was how I met Leo; in between churches and disillusioned after the breakdown of my friendship at the previous church.

Leo was a nice guy, a Christian. He had recently come back from a mission trip in the Middle East, and was somewhere in between finding a purpose for his life and settling down. I immediately recognised that he was also struggling with his sexuality and had identity issues. And what should have been warning signs became strangely comforting; at least he was someone who would know how I used to feel, or so I thought.

Well, we 'clicked,' had a couple of meals together and ended up sleeping together. I genuinely wanted to help him, but completely fell into temptation.

Nobody knew about Leo's personal struggles with his sexual identity except our friend, the minister. He feared being rejected or even worse, ostracised. Maybe he did not believe himself to be a new creation in Christ, or maybe he had not taken his broken gender and sexuality to God. I, on the other hand, had now fallen back into the habit of the past life, the one I led without Jesus. It was a real mess and it did not stop there.

It was all wrong and we both knew it. We were both lonely and insecure, and all the changes we had recently been through became a lethal combination for compromise. Our trust in God was gone; we were trusting in each other now.

Leo and I lasted a year. Impatience brings such great sadness and fear. I spent a year of hiding from everyone; family, friends and the wider church friendships I had. He was only my 'flatmate', we would tell people – but it was all a lie. It was terrible having to avoid others in fear of being caught, or confronted. They must have known, or maybe not, or maybe they did not know how to help.

My journey back to God was even tougher. I had to forgive myself for what I had done, even though I knew that God had already forgiven me. I was so angry with myself for wasting this year in sin and compromise. I knew God was not angry at me, but I wanted him to be; I felt that I deserved his anger. But he was the same loving Father, waiting for me, the prodigal, to return.

So it was true, I was not in a particularly good place when I first met Samantha. And now here I was at James and Roelene's wedding reception, sat at the singles table with a beautiful girl, Samantha, on my right, and Leo on my left. Yes, he was also invited to the wedding.

All through the meal God was whispering in my ear: 'Choose! You choose! Life with her and me, or him!'

Leo watched the whole thing unfold. He was just as much living a compromise. It could not have been easy for him. What a predicament I was in, and not a soul knew about it. The good thing was that I never let my cover slip about Leo to Samantha. I just knew that I needed to get away with God and make some big decisions about this mess I was navigating.

CHAPTER 20
THE LISTENER
+ + +

I went home from the wedding that night with a heavy heart. I knew that I had a choice to make that would define the next season of my life. I felt like it was a watershed moment, a critical point on my journey. Should I stay with Leo and remain in the weirdly secure life of compromise we had created, or should I end it? Ending it would be a choice to run back to God and to face up to my sin, and open the way to developing a relationship with Samantha. Whatever I did, there would be pain for others and myself.

I cried and prayed and settled it. I chose God and Samantha. It was hard to tell Leo, and he did not take it well, even though throughout the wedding reception he had been watching us. He suspected something was happening before his very eyes, and was right. So we had to agree: we were never right, should never have been together, and we both belonged to God, to whom we should now return fully and start over again. He left the flat and I broke all contact with him. It should never have been.

I had to humble myself before God. The guilt I suffered took a long time to go, or maybe I should say it took me a long time to give up the guilt and fully receive God's gracious forgiveness. Not only had I left the church angry, discontent and impatient, I had just had a year of compromised living, which had caused a lot of hurt, and I now had to make things right with others and with God.

I also resolved that I had to tell Samantha as soon as possible.

During the week after the wedding, I invited Samantha for breakfast at a café in town. We were both so nervous. I really liked her, but just had to come clean about my true condition. I still had to tell her; in part because I was so scared she would hear it from someone else in the singles group as Leo had now gone to stay with another friend of hers.

I told her the whole story about Leo and me, all of it. I had to risk it. I liked her very much and even if it meant that I would lose her, I still had tell her. And if our relationship was to go any further, I didn't want to risk hurting her by any skeletons falling out of my cupboard down the line. I knew that she would have to be of some character not to run for miles when she heard all that I was about to say!

We did not eat a thing. She just listened. She had empathy with my pain from her experience with her gay family member, which gave her a real insight and understanding of me. Amazingly, she did not judge me. Wow! Such grace.

To finish my story that breakfast-time, I added that I liked her very much. She was a very special girl and I did not want her to get hurt, or for me to get hurt – but for us to continue with this friendship any further we needed to take it before the Lord in prayer.

Funnily enough, I had bumped into Samantha's ma in a coffee shop a week or so before the wedding. She was so glad to see me and mentioned that she had missed me at church and that I had been in her thoughts and prayers for a while now. Little did she know where I had been. Looking back on it all now, I can see how it all helped to prepare room for me in her family's life.

Samantha baked me a cake for my birthday, and I took her flowers when I returned the empty cake tin. It was also my first visit to her parents' house. I think they saw it coming before we did. Her mother told me later that as she prayed for me God had shown her that I was to become a son in their house and that she was to love me. Talk about God preparing the way!

We didn't see each other for the next two weeks, in part so we could get some clarity on our new relationship. I remember meeting up with François, praying fiercely in those weeks for her and me, for us, for my future wife – or so I hoped by then. My earnest prayer was that God would give me a wife who would be a listener, someone with whom I could share my whole heart in total openness. I had finished with compromise and cover-ups. I wanted to live in the freedom of an open, loving relationship with someone who would hear me and still love me.

The next time we met was at my flat. I'd baked a banana loaf because she was coming straight from swimming at the gym and I knew she would be hungry. I remember having her sat next to me on the sofa and sheepishly trying to make light conversation. I asked, 'Erm, what does your name mean, then, Samantha?'

Her answer blew me away: 'Samantha means listener,' she said. Wow! Something just resonated in my spirit. In that moment I knew she was my wife. The last thing I had so desperately asked God for was a wife who would be a listener; and here she was, 'the listener'. This was too good to be a coincidence.

By now we had known each other about four weeks and I told her straight, 'I am going to marry you. You tell your parents if you want, but before long I will come and ask them to let me have you as my wife.' Why she wasn't completely freaked out by my boldness, or rather my conceitedness, still puzzles me today. But what followed was a great courtship.

We spent a lot of time together after that day, talking about everything. We spent late nights on my balcony overlooking the city or sometimes just walking about window shopping after a movie or a meal out. Late one evening we strolled past a local florist; it was well past midnight and they were just having a consignment delivered, so I bought her flowers in the middle of the night. We were in love and it was very special. We shared our dreams and expectations for life and the future. It was awesome. Chatting came naturally with her, and I could just be myself.

But as it is with this life, challenges soon came.

The word got out – well, two words actually: the word about Samantha and I being together, but also the word about how I had been living with Leo for the previous year. It had consequences, like these things do. Sin is sin and there are always consequences; it just seems that some sins have greater consequences, especially sexual sins.

Through it all, I lost some credibility as a Christian, which really upset me. It was all very painful and I had to take the consequences and responsibility for my wrongdoing. But I also had to make a stand for I knew that God was doing a new thing in me and us, and that was far more precious than the opposition we were facing. Some of our friends became very negative about Samantha and I. Everyone had an opinion, like they do in situations like this. As they say, an opinion is like a nose, we all have one, and we don't need two! But we were getting plenty directed at us.

We had to confront one close friend of Samantha's in particular. Leo had confided in her after we broke up about living with me the previous year. She was concerned and had a right to be, but it was crossing a line. So I arranged for her to meet us at my flat so we could get it all resolved. In the end I had to say to her that if she couldn't bless or support what was growing between Samantha and me, then she had no right to be part of it. We had to stand our ground. Maybe I was a bit heavy-handed but it was the truth. Our relationship was fragile in those early days and we wanted to protect our love. So, even though it was painful, Samantha had to let her close friend go.

The sin Leo and I committed had so many consequences for us, and for others. So my prayer was, 'Forgive me, Lord, for the mess we left, and please Lord, help me to sort this out!' Never forget that sin carries consequences and the pain endures. But God's amazing grace will pull you through if you will face up to the sin and work it through with God and the people concerned.

It's funny how relationships polarise when you become a fixed item with someone. Some take a position of not being happy about the relationship, and others cheer you on! Some now feel they cannot be your friend anymore because you have a new one. It's strange what goes on in people's minds when you enter a settled relationship with someone.

I guess it's the principle of 'leaving and cleaving' at work (see Genesis 2:24). You can't grab onto something or someone new without letting go of something else, to use the analogy of the trapeze artists. We felt like we were letting go of some relationships so that we could grasp firmly hold of our new one. But just now we were flying through the air, feeling light-hearted and happy but also a little scared. But we knew that trust had to be the foundation of our relationship, so held on to each other and God as we hurtled through the air into our future together.

CHAPTER 21
MARRIED
+ + +

Three months into our relationship, I desperately wanted to propose to Samantha. It was just right. But I'd had a trip booked to visit my family back in the Western Cape for a long time, so found myself jetting off and leaving her in Namibia.

I was especially looking forward to seeing *Ouma*. Of all my family she was the one I could confide in, and who had stood by me without judging me all my life – and I was now thirty-one. I bought a beautiful piece of agate from a gem shop in Windhoek for her, as she so loved stone formations. I also had a question for her burning in my heart.

We were all so happy and excited to see each other. My family had heard of all the change in my life and I could not wait to share more with them. Both my ma and little sister had since come to faith in Jesus, and the news about me meeting a girl was well-received.

It was a well-deserved break and I got to see all the family and friends I wanted to see. I then spent the last three days with *Ouma* with this burning question inside of me.

On the last day, I made her a hot drink and took it to her room. As I sat on the side of her bed after an afternoon's rest, she suddenly sat up and turned to me. She asked, 'What is so difficult for you to ask me, my child?'

I almost fell off her bed! Still baffled by her intuition, the words just tumbled out of my mouth. 'I want to ask Samantha to marry me, and could I have your engagement ring to do so?'

Immediately she got up, walked over to a dresser, took the ring out and looked at me. 'I was wondering who I was to give this to,' she said with a smile. And it was mine. How awesome was God in this provision for me? Thank you, Lord, for having an *ouma* who had a strong faith in God and who never failed to love me!

Once back in Windhoek, I was burning to propose to Samantha. You know how it is when you can't wait to ask, or to give someone something special? I was giddy with excitement one minute then overcome with fears of possible rejection the next. What if she said 'no'? I just had to risk it!

So one afternoon, I did a kind of trial run with her. On my way back from the city one day, I passed a small craft stall at the local African market and saw some beautiful adjustable brass bangles. I bought a couple and on returning to the flat, I found Samantha in the kitchen. 'Feeling the waters', I slipped a bangle on her arm and said sheepishly, 'So if I asked you to marry me, would you?'

'Yes,' she laughed. 'Of course I would, you silly!'

Joy, unspeakable joy, followed. I just had to keep my pose. This is no way to propose, I thought, and left it there.

I had decided to use a local jeweller to redesign *Ouma's* ring to suit Samantha's taste; meanwhile, I hatched a plan for a proper proposal. A romantic lunch was booked at Gathemann's, a great contemporary German restaurant in the city. After ordering some drinks, I excused myself from the table to go to the gents, but it was a ruse because I still had to pick up the ring from the jewellers, just round the corner. I ran there like the wind and Samantha had no idea where I had gone. I was somewhat out of breath when I re-emerged from the gents. She looked at me and said, 'That was rather long! Are you OK?'

'I'm fine,' I replied, while subtly slipping the ring box under her napkin on the table.

Our food came and we just kept on chatting. I was consumed with excitement as the sun streamed through into the first-floor terrace where we were sitting. The plates left the table. Then she discovered it. The box, the ring!

A very formal 'Will you marry me?' followed. And she said 'yes'! I was overcome by emotion. We kissed. So happy, so grateful! It was official.

Oh, by the way, talking about doing things the right way, I didn't. I only went to ask her parents after I had proposed to her – whoops! I should have found out how to do it right, but this is stuff you are supposed to learn from your own dad.

The following afternoon we went to join her parents for lunch. On arrival, her ma said, 'You will never believe what happened at church today. Someone came up to me and asked whether you had proposed to Samantha.' I had to bite my tongue. Oh no! The story had leaked out; now I wasn't sure what to do. Eventually, some hours later after they had retired to bed, I walked into their bedroom and asked them for Samantha's hand. They didn't look too surprised, although my mother-in-law did say, 'Well, I suppose we can't say no!' She was teasing me a little. We all knew that it was not really a matter of asking their permission; what we wanted was their blessing, and they gave it.

The wedding plans were set in motion and many of our friends helped out. An amazing couple made their home available for my family to stay in when they came up from South Africa, and so many others contributed generously with their talents and abilities. It was great!

We decided to have the ceremony in the garden centre where I'd had the first hair salon, Co-Hairance. I still had good relationships with the owners and they made it special for us. In the middle of the garden centre was a lovely gazebo that served as the 'roof over our heads' during the ceremony.

While we were in Cape Town, on a visit to formally introduce Samantha to my family, she found a beautiful dress and all the girly accessories she wanted – it was so easy. The family instantly loved her and everything just fell into place: the flowers, photographer, music, venue, reception, a great menu, and we were expecting fantastic weather.

My family arrived the day before, and we all had a lovely meal together.

On the morning of the wedding I felt rested, got up and found myself standing in front of the wardrobe admiring my wedding attire, when a wave of fear came over me. It's important I share this with you because it is a crucial part of my journey.

I stood there frozen in fear for a moment, with this thought in my mind: 'What if the sex doesn't work?' I had never been in a committed relationship with a girl before, and had never been that sexually attracted to them, and I didn't want my relationship with Samantha to be just flesh and lust-driven like I had occasionally experienced before. I prayed, 'Lord, you know I love her more than my own life now, but what if the sex does not work?' It had always been easy with the men, for that was all I was used to. But this was new and the thought of me being that intimate and tender with a girl was filling me with an irrational but very real fear. It felt like my lungs were being squeezed by a large fist, which expelled the air from them.

I called out to God, 'Father, help me! Please help me!' And this comforting scripture came to mind in that instant: 'What father would give his child a scorpion when he asked for an egg?' (see Luke 11:11–13). I pondered on what that scripture meant and the most amazing peacefulness followed as I realised: an egg is life and a scorpion, death. It all made sense now; I must trust God for this, for our sex life, and believe it would be life-giving and life-enriching.

There was a sudden knock on the door, which made me jump. It was my best man, François. What a great friend he had been to me over the years. We got dressed together and he prayed with me before we left for the venue.

I stood at the entrance greeting our family, friends and guests as they came in. There was so much love there. Then with butterflies of excitement in my stomach, I took my place at the front.

The air was thick with expectation for the presence of God and for Samantha's arrival. And then she came. She looked awesome – I know I'm biased, but she did! Here she was, my bride, my wife. I just cried with happiness and deep gratitude because none of this would have been possible if it hadn't been for what Jesus had done for me on the cross. His love and mercy towards me were beyond words that day. Thank you, Father!

I stood there and allowed the love and gratitude to flow over me. It had all started the day I met Jesus, and the new man I became was now no longer alone. Here I was with everyone who was dear to me at the time. Adopted into the family of God, no more an orphan spirit, but completely accepted. And next to me was my Samantha, my 'listener', my Eve, the one prepared for me.

Unbeknown to us, some of Samantha's work friends had prepared a special song for our wedding day, and they very cleverly slipped it into the order of service – a song for us, about love. Now, there are very few things that are as touching as a bunch of African women singing from their hearts in perfect harmony. It was simply beautiful. There was not a dry eye in the audience. My ma, who was sitting a couple of feet behind me, had to lean forward to stuff a handful of tissues in my hand. More tears of gratefulness followed. *Husband and wife!* I thought, pinching myself.

Next, there was tea and coffee and light refreshment for all those who came. The hugs and kisses of congratulation were profuse and then we were soon off for photos at an old industrial disused power station. We wanted some interesting wedding photos and thought the industrial venue would make for a good contrast. It was the artist in me expressing itself.

Then the reception followed, held at the old German colonial Pension (boutique hotel) called *Kleines Heim*. We had given it lots of thought and had decided not to have a head table. Ours consisted of just really close friends, brothers and sisters. I wanted everyone to feel safe and I wanted them close. It was good that way. Everyone sat round big tables with white tablecloths that gently moved in the breeze. They were arranged around a pool under an open heaven. The gently waving palm trees, clear skies, excellent food and good music made for a late night of dancing with some awesome company. What more could I ask for?

Absolute bliss!

CHAPTER 22
THAILAND TO DEWSBURY
+ + +

We honeymooned in Thailand. And we were ready for it; getting married is really hard work and we were exhausted! Our destination was Chiang Mai in the north of Thailand, an area surrounded by lush forests and small villages. We stayed in a beautiful hotel in the city.

There we made love for the first time, and wow – it worked! I mean, sex worked and I just couldn't get over how beautiful my wife was. God had been so faithful to us. There was trust, tenderness and kindness. God's grace was over us. God was in it. I now fully understood that sex was God's idea and that he had always meant for it to be expressed by lovers like us within the bond of marriage.

We then flew south to the island of Ko Samui off the southern coast for a few days. It was a beautiful resort in a beachside setting, such a contrast to the lush jungle of the north. Then we spent our last four days in Bangkok, frequenting the local markets, sight-seeing and enjoying the food served from the riverboats – it certainly is a city of contrast where elephants and cars, bicycles and tuk-tuks share the same motorway. Extraordinary!

One day in Bangkok we met a tailor who asked us whether we were Christians. He was searching for God and had a sister who had become a Christian recently while watching Christian TV. She had shared the message of Christ with him, and left him with so many questions about our faith. It was an everyday opportunity to share the love of Jesus with a stranger. When we went back for a second fitting, he brought his whole family along and we ended up in their home and praying for his young son, who was born deaf. What a privilege to spend time with them. We received Christmas cards from them in the years that followed.

Thailand was a beautiful experience, except for one thing: the sex trade. Seeing it at first-hand shocked me. Mere children were being hawked as prostitutes and rent boys in all the bars; it was appalling and seemingly an accepted part of the tourist industry. It broke my heart. I knew it was not God's best for them or for anyone involved in what was essentially a criminal industry of abuse. There were little girls working as prostitutes and little boys who had been thrown away by their families because there was simply not enough money to feed them, only to become rent boys or later, lady-boys. Many were trying to make ends meet either for their families or trying to raise money for possible sex changes later in life. And all so that someone would love them one day. We had so much in common.

Something had to be done. 'How, Lord?' I prayed. I knew they needed the message of Jesus' redeeming love, and I had to take it to them somehow one day.

Soon after we got back to Namibia, a letter arrived for Samantha. It said that she had received a general invitation from a recruitment company in the UK. At that time the National Health Service were desperate for medical staff and doctors in particular. It just so happened that Samantha had studied at a university that was recognised by the British General Medical Council, so was a prime candidate.

We had previously thought that South Africa, Canada or Australia were possible options for Samantha to go and specialise.

But this offer for the UK felt right to us, so she applied and was quickly accepted.

Immediately we told our families, friends, my staff and clients that we were going to leave for the UK. A colleague and good friend of mine wanted to keep the business going and took all my staff on, which was a big relief. Thanks, Lord; that was such an answer to my prayers. We set a date for a general sale of our possessions in the flat and the entire contents sold in one weekend. The only things I kept were paintings, rugs and books. We reasoned that as the décor and furniture in the apartment was all to my taste, it would give Samantha and I an opportunity to start afresh when we got our new home abroad. Things were moving fast and we were off, stepping out in faith on a new adventure together.

Technically, we had no confirmation or security that Samantha definitely had a job in the UK as yet. But it looked promising and I had always wanted to work abroad. I reflected back on getting the application for Toni & Guy all those years ago, long before I had come to know the Lord. But even more than that, I had this dream to take my life, my story and all that God had done for me into the rest of the world and this was going to be the opportunity – or so I hoped and prayed. Only time would tell.

The date came closer and closer to our departure, and still we had no word of her work or the necessary entry permits that would enable us to enter the UK and work. More prayer, more trust. We just had to wait on God and his timing. We spent some time with Samantha's parents, and even though we were sad to leave them, they were extremely supportive of us. It must have been hard for them.

Our friends at church were also kind enough to do a communal goodbye for us. It was an opportunity for us to be prayed for by

147

the church and sent on our way with blessing. It was good to be sent rather than just be leaving.

Still no news of a job or the permits, but our flights were booked; we were just trusting God it would work out. We combined our departure with a short visit to my family in South Africa before we flew from Cape Town to London. It was lovely to see them. Then on the next-to-last day of our stay, the day before we flew, the permits came, and Samantha's work details. Phew! What a test of faith that was.

Because the work permit and paperwork came through so close to the date of our departure, we had no idea where the place we were heading for was; we just knew we were arriving at Heathrow Airport and would go from there. Talk about moving blind! Our destination was the town of Dewsbury, where the locum agency had found a job for Samantha, at Dewsbury and District Hospital to be precise.

I had been to the UK before some years earlier, but this was Samantha's first time. My visit had been with Ma to visit my younger sister, Anna. So much restoration had followed in our relationship since I met Jesus. Anna was working as a PA for someone who had bought a beautiful estate in Surrey with eleven acres of gorgeous countryside. We had done some of the tourist things: the sights of London, then Scotland, which included the Edinburgh Fringe, an arts and cultural festival, Inverness, Fort William and Oban on the stunning west coast. It was a fantastic trip. I didn't remember seeing Dewsbury, though. Where was this Dewsbury, West Yorkshire? We were soon to find out.

We arrived in the UK on Valentine's Day 2003, very tired and a bit lost. Not being as aware as we should have been, we ended up with separate immigration officers at border control, which is how you do it in Africa. The outcome was that Samantha, having had all the paperwork with her, got the relevant stamp in her passport, and I, on the other hand, got a six months' visitor's visa. All very complicated.

We had left South Africa in late summer, where the temperatures can reach forty degrees Celsius, and arrived in London where it was minus six. Chilly! We literally walked out of the terminal building and went to find out how we got to Dewsbury. By coach was the answer. So we booked our place for the journey north, which took a very long time – eight and a half hours to be precise, and that was only to Leeds. We then had to get the local bus to Dewsbury. We had stopped at many villages, towns and cities on the way. At least we got to see lots of the UK. Eventually, the bus finally dropped us off at the entrance to the hospital where we would be staying. We were exhausted!

Dewsbury is small market town in West Yorkshire, in the north of England. It had boomed during the industrial revolution in Victorian England, making its money in textile manufacturing. But it had since fallen into poverty and despair. What remained was a town with some history and many beautiful buildings, but with very little money.

After we arrived at the hospital, some arrangements had to be made by the accommodation officer for us, and the key had to be fetched for our accommodation. I stood outside the hospital, waiting patiently in the freezing cold, while Samantha sorted it. I had almost turned blue by the time she returned some forty-five minutes later! The accommodation officer had left to go home, as it was Valentine's Day and a Friday. So, the wonderful alternative we were presented with was to bunk in the singles' accommodation block for the night. Not ideal for newly-weds like us!

It took some initiative, searching a few storerooms and

cupboards in the single quarters to find an extra mattress, which we ended up putting on the floor and standing the single bed up against the wall. And that was it.

Exhausted, we tumbled into our makeshift bed. What a day it had been. We never expected it to end quite like this. But here we were in Dewsbury, wondering how things would now unfold in our new home.

CHAPTER 23
CLOSER TO THE DREAM
+ + +

Good morning, Dewsbury!

It was a dark and cold February day. We had hoped to get ourselves orientated, but there was little time because Samantha had to start working immediately on night shifts. Talk about going in at the deep end! We had a new job, new home, in a new country, with new people and a new system of doing things. What a challenge we had. It was both scary and exciting. What a roller coaster ride of emotions.

The day Samantha was to begin her nights, she was in tears. It was a mixture of fear and homesickness, which I guess was understandable. I mean, we had anticipated some homesickness, just not this soon. Isn't there supposed to be a honeymoon period at times like this? Apparently not! So I encouraged her to persevere, always confident that Dewsbury would not be forever, it was just the starting point of our life in the UK.

My passport status prohibited me from working, which I had initially seen as a problem. But I soon realised that it was something of a blessing. We had never lived in this First World system before, where Samantha's good salary actually released me to run the house and get to know how society worked. So I became the expert in buses, bins, bills, trains, shopping, local government and the National Health Service – a proper househusband!

We ended up living in married accommodation, which consisted of a small bungalow next to the hospital. We were so ignorant about how to run a home in the UK that we kept the gas range burning for two weeks, heating up pans of water to fill a bath, only to find out later how the central heating system and boiler worked. Praise God for the postman, who enlightened us about it. We had to laugh!

Samantha got to meet a lot of new medics from all over the world and we soon got to know many of them. We discovered that most of them were in the same boat as us. It's strange how similar circumstances bring people together; we were all in a new country, a new job, a new culture, and needed new friends.

Meanwhile, I had a lot of time on my hands. I mean, how often can you clean a two-bedroomed, semi-detached, NHS bungalow like ours? How often can you go shopping? And the truth is, I quickly got to know the local area. I discovered Dewsbury Market, which is quite famous locally for its food, and gradually explored the neighbouring towns and cities, like Leeds. One thing I also began to wonder about was, how do you start looking for a church family to belong to?

Unfortunately, I still could not work without getting my passport status changed. So I got an appointment with the Passport Office in Liverpool and was hoping to have it all sorted soon.

I also filled some of my time reading a book on how to spend more intimate time with God in order to get to know him better. Those first six months waiting for the passport and job opportunities actually proved to be a very valuable and amazingly close time with him. I began to appreciate the privilege I had in the midst of all the change to 'settle' with Jesus and dig deeper into our relationship in order to prepare for our life in the UK.

One day on my travels, I stumbled across a bookstore

attached to a small church in the town. I had been praying for a church family locally, for we did not have a car yet, and I was rather daunted by the fact that there are literally thousands of churches in the UK from every denomination you can think of. So where do you start? But this one just felt right, so we decided to give it a try.

The church was called Dewsbury Gospel Church. We soon made some friends and had good times together which further helped us settle into UK life. One quite unique thing about that little church was that they had their own private digital radio station broadcasting across the West Yorkshire region. This led to a wonderful opportunity: I was asked to share my story on air. I couldn't believe it; here I was talking about how Jesus had turned my life around, and now West Yorkshire could be listening!

On one of my days exploring the city of Leeds, I stumbled across a Toni & Guy hair salon. How strange to be stood there. It was over twelve years since I had got application forms to go and work there, and now here I was on their doorstep. I stood in front of the shop, trying to be as incognito as possible, and prayed fervently for an opportunity to work there!

In the meantime, I had to go to the Passport Office in Liverpool to get my status sorted out. This was faith in action for me, but it paid off and I got the permissions I needed to be able to work.

Not long after, I took Samantha to Leeds for a look around on one of her days off and walked past the Toni & Guy salon again. Amazingly, there was a vacancy in the window, so I went straight in and was accepted for an interview. The interview could not come soon enough for me. I took Samantha as my model and did my best haircut and got the job. Awesome!

Then, just a few days later, I had a call from the manager to say that the stylist I was replacing had now decided not to leave!

She, understandably, preferred to keep an existing member of staff rather than employing someone new. I was momentarily deflated until she then went on to say that her friend, who owned the Toni & Guy salon in Harrogate, North Yorkshire, was looking for someone and she would recommend me to her if I fancied applying.

I explored things and found that Harrogate is a beautiful and affluent spa town, situated just north of Leeds and about thirty-five miles away from Dewsbury. It was certainly within the wider region we knew Samantha would be working in. So I went for the interview and got the job.

Samantha's six-month locum position at Dewsbury was coming to an end, which meant she had to decide whether to renew it or not. It seemed the perfect time to look for a move and, if possible, to Harrogate. We still didn't have a car so we prayed earnestly that God would provide her with a job in Harrogate so that we could move there and both walk to work. And believe it or not, an opening came up for a position in the Accident and Emergency at Harrogate and District Hospital. It was a gap made for Samantha as far as we were concerned!

By the time we heard that Samantha had got the job in Harrogate I'd been commuting there for a couple of months. But now we could move. We just saw it as another miracle of God's provision for us. We looked at rented accommodation and decided on an apartment in an old Victorian house. It was situated on the Stray, a lovely open communal green park with tree-lined borders in this beautiful town. Wonderful! This was just right for us.

However, getting it proved quite a challenge, because having only been in the UK for a few months, the letting agents were sceptical about our credibility as tenants. We had no credit record and they couldn't access our bank account because it was overseas. Ultimately we had to ask another medic who Samantha knew to stand as a guarantor for us; meanwhile, our friends from the church in Dewsbury put us up until the flat eventually came through. It proved to be another walk of faith but we got to Harrogate. It was such a great relief when it all came together. Through tears and trust, God had proved himself good to us again.

We had nothing in the form of furniture to take with us at this point, as the bungalow in Dewsbury was furnished by the hospital. We ordered some furniture from a local store, just to hear that it had to be made and it would be three months before delivery. So, we got a mattress to fit the bed and, with the bedding we'd brought with us, at least we could sleep.

The rest of the terraced house was owned by a lovely Jewish man whose father lived below us from time to time when he wasn't abroad. He was very friendly to us. What must he have thought when we moved in? An empty apartment with a mattress on the floor; it baffled him. We soon became close friends with him and his extended family.

We had no television, which the licensing authorities found very peculiar, even to the point of wanting to investigate our home. But we had deliberately decided not to have one; it seemed strange to start with a television if you don't have a table and chairs to sit at.

However, our lovely neighbour offered us an old black and white one because he had five – yes, five – TVs! Very sweet of him, we thought. He spent hours in our kitchen chatting about life and we shared our faith in Jesus with him. He even invited us to his place to watch the God channel; he found these born-again Christians very intriguing. There was a permission to share our faith, a favour in this friendship, which was wonderful.

We were soon settled in our new jobs. It's strange how quickly one's world settles down into a routine. Samantha could walk to work and we ended up getting her a good bicycle as the trip to the hospital took literally five minutes. And my work was only a short walk away. I had to start building a clientele as I was a brand-new team member in the salon, but met a whole bunch of wonderful people in a very short space of time and was enjoying things.

Now we were living locally, it was time to think about church again. I spoke to God about it and during the following week, three people from the same church came to me as new 'walk-in' clients. So we decided to investigate because we needed and wanted to be part of a community of Christians again. And what we found there was a real home from home.

For us, the church is where relationships are made, dreams are shared, and we can grow through hearing and doing what God's Word teaches us to do. No church is ever perfect – especially after we walk in! It is just a community of imperfect people who are each in a process of outworking their faith journey with God. And we had found one that fitted us well.

One of the junior pastors of the church had done some training with a larger church in West Yorkshire called Life Church. We visited there from time to time, and it became an inspiring model for us as a local church in Harrogate. Changes were being made to the way the church operated and not everyone liked it, but we loved it. So we threw our weight behind the leadership team and their vision. I ended up serving in many areas as a volunteer and running multiple departments of church life. We served on the host team, facilitated a small group, and I got involved in the running of an Alpha course (www.alpha.org). I loved helping the new believers start their Christian journey with strength and purpose. I even got involved in doing the hair and make-up for the media department. Life became very full, and it took some juggling to manage my time.

Through all this, I was still in a process of finding my fit, my niche, outworking my dream of helping those who came from a similar background to mine. I had the dream in my heart but not yet a plan of how to outwork it. Meanwhile, serving in all those areas definitely helped me find exactly what I wanted to do, and gave God the opportunity to work on my character.

Time rolled on and Samantha's twelve-month contract working in Harrogate Accident and Emergency department came to an end. By this time, she was desperate to pursue her dream, which was to become an anaesthetist.

One Tuesday afternoon, I had a new client in the chair. We introduced ourselves, and as we chatted I ended up sharing a little about Samantha's dream. I even had the boldness to say that she was willing to take any job in the hospital and wait until a vacancy occurred in anaesthetics. My client, Melanie, looked at me strangely and explained that she was one of the consultant anaesthetists who sat on the panel of interviewers for new applicants. The coincidence was freaking us both out, I think.

Only God could have orchestrated this. Did my boldness pay off? Yes! For at the next set of interviews, Samantha got the job and got to meet Melanie, her new boss. Soon after, she received the training number needed to enter the rota to become an anaesthetic consultant. Her training was going take seven years on the West Yorkshire rotation, starting in Harrogate. What more could we have asked for? Thank you, Father!

I was making progress too. I had been working as a stylist for Toni & Guy for a while now, and the next step was to become a top stylist. The test involved me doing ten specific haircuts and some creative styling, which would be judged by two art directors of the company, one of them being my existing boss. My relationships at church proved to be invaluable, because I knew I could find ten clients who would model for me. I had the use of the salon to prepare all the models while Samantha and our friends, Ian and Sarah, helped out. When the judges arrived, we served them with strawberries and champagne – not a bribe, you understand, but all part of the creative experience I crafted for them. And happily, it all went well and they passed me and I proceeded to become a top stylist.

We spent a week down in London, sightseeing and celebrating after all the hard work that went into preparing for it. I was living the dream, the Toni & Guy dream. But I still had a bigger dream in my heart, a dream far larger than doing hair.

CHAPTER 24
CLARIFYING THE FOCUS
+ + +

Reflecting back on my life up to this point utterly amazed me; it was so completely different to the place I started from, such a transformation, and for one reason only: I met Jesus and decided to live my life with him. How could I now keep quiet about the wonderful things God had done for me?

My story had already helped some people to make better choices, particularly about their gender identity issues, for which I was grateful. But I felt as if I was only just scratching the surface. Deep in my heart a dream had incubated and was now growing larger and larger. I wanted to help more people; the freedom I had found must be proclaimed to all with similar challenges to mine. It was like a volcano gently gathering heat, deep in the earth; I knew one day this thing was going to erupt and become a tool in God's hand to help many more people. But I felt so inadequate still.

The more the dream grew, the more I began to seriously think about taking a year out to get some proper biblical training. I loved God and his Word, but knew I needed a far better grasp of it before the dream could become a reality. I also knew my character still needed working on; it needed shaping and purifying to ensure it would be a safe vessel for the dream once it was birthed.

As I mentioned earlier, our church in Harrogate had strong

links with Life Church in Bradford. So we decided to go and see for ourselves what this church was like that others spoke so highly of. We went a couple of times on a Sunday evening, and for the first time in a long time, felt like we had come home. It consisted of a large and lively multifaceted congregation. There were young and old, many nationalities and a genuine atmosphere of unity around a desire to reach the community for Jesus.

On one of those visits we discovered they ran a Leadership Academy, which was a one or two-year full-time course. The course was designed to give the students a good, solid foundation in Christian doctrine, develop their leadership skills and hone their characters. It sounded like the ideal place for me to get the training I was looking for.

Samantha and I prayerfully considered it, especially the financial and other practical implications, and decided to risk it. I applied and went for an interview, then had to wait a few days before hearing if I had been accepted – in part because they wanted to take references from our current church leaders. Those few days were nerve-racking and served to cause all my fears of rejection to surface again. I still had some trust issues to deal with and also needed to deal with some deep feelings of inadequacy. Insecurity is terribly debilitating; it actually proved to me I needed this course to help me work it all through.

Doubts and fears were dispelled when my acceptance letter arrived. Wow! What a relief, I thought.

So here I was, leaving a good job again. My boss was reluctant to let me go, and was even kind enough to keep my job open if I ever felt like coming back. I suspect that had more to do with the money I was earning for them than my charming personality! But I had to go and follow my dream.

The saddest part was leaving all my clients behind. I remember thinking, this is becoming a pattern: I spent five years working in Cape Town, then eight years in Namibia, and now three years in the UK. Each time I had met so many people, journeyed with them for a while and shared my story of meeting Jesus with them, and then it was time to move on again. Many of them became friends who I saw every few weeks. We talked about everything, even the big taboo subjects like sex, politics and religion. We often spoke about God, and the salon would go noticeably quiet as everyone listened. People are always searching, whether they will admit it or not. They are in what the Bible calls 'the valley of decision' (Joel 3:14), a place we all find ourselves in at some point in life; a place where we get to choose or reject God and the wonderful life he offers.

My parting prayer was that all the conversations I had enjoyed with my almost 350 clients would live on in their memories, and play a part in helping them to choose Jesus like I did. But as for me, I had to move on from the salon, for the dream in my heart was burning passionately.

I started the one-year full-time course in September of 2006. Each day I commuted from Harrogate to Bradford with two other students – Owen, who was Welsh-English, and Aisling, who was Irish-English. The three of us made a cosmopolitan contribution to the year group and became affectionately known as the 'Harrogate Bus'.

The year group was amazing. We were fifty-two students from eleven different countries, aged from nineteen to sixty-two. Most of us were financially challenged, but used this opportunity to share our skills and talents to serve each other, and God provided the rest. You have to help where you can. One of the ladies was a good cook and she always had some cakes or bread ready in our breaks. Equally, I could give haircuts away, so by the time I had finished the course, I had built up a great clientele, as most of my fellow classmates went back into full-time employment and could then afford to pay me!

The Leadership Studies course helped me to develop my dream of helping others who come from a similar background to me, not something many churches do well. I don't want to be overly critical, but in my experience many churches are ill-equipped to deal with issues of gender and sexuality and I wanted to fix that; to develop a ministry that would genuinely help those trapped in same-sex attraction issues and gender dysfunction.

The year at the Leadership Academy was awesome! So much so I am tempted to give you a summary of all the great teaching we received and the character development challenges we worked through. But space does not permit. However, the programme is still running and you can always explore it for yourself by visiting www.lifechurchhome.com/college.

One big lesson I learned was that everyone finds their purpose in life once they have a living relationship with God. Until then, you are on your own, doing it in your own strength. But once you meet Jesus, everything changes. You then live in the flow of God's amazing grace, which is his underserved favour. We could never earn it and certainly don't deserve it, but he showers us with it every day that we decide to walk in step with his Holy Spirit, who now lives within us. It is an amazing way to live – the only way.

As the course unfolded, God touched my life in many ways and I was particularly gripped by the teaching on living a God-centred life. This spoke to me clearly about the need for people to make God central to every area of life, not just certain aspects of it. It was then that God started to clarify for me what the dream in my heart, in connection with living a life of God-centred identity, gender and sexuality, should actually look like.

Let me personalise my thought process for you: I realised that after I met Christ and entered into relationship with my heavenly Father, his Spirit started permeating every area and facet of my life as I allowed him to. That included my gender and sexuality. Maybe this was more pronounced in my life, in that I had so much sexual brokenness and gender dysfunction in my past. But I came to recognise that his will for me regarding gender was to become a man of God, with my sexuality held within the safe, loving boundaries of his Word and Spirit, and for sex to be kept within marriage as he intended. Only then would I be living a truly God-centred life.

That personal revelation and my decision to fully align my life with God's will for me as a man, is where my freedom comes from. I am free to be all he created me to be. And my dream was that thousands of others would find the same freedom as me.

All it now needed was a vehicle and a plan. The vehicle was the ministry God then birthed in my heart, now known as Gender Plus, and the plan… well, you are reading part of it!

CHAPTER 25
REALISING THE DREAM
+ + +

The ministry, Gender Plus, was born one night when I woke in the early hours with the name on my heart. It was that simple. In my mind it suddenly clicked that in all the debate about gender and sexuality, everything works when we have Gender Plus Jesus; when we have Gender Plus surrendering it all to him. When I give God my all, my sexuality, identity and gender, all of me, things change and wholeness can be achieved.

Soon after, I spoke to the leadership at church about my embryonic ideas and was encouraged to write my story down. Yes, I thought, why not write a book, grow a ministry and develop a website that relates to all things gender? And so it all began, and you are reading that book!

After the Leadership Academy course ended, I continued to work with some of the church pastors very discreetly. They connected me with a few guys in the church who were struggling with issues like my old ones. In this way, Gender Plus became a reality, an actual ministry of a local church. I was also asked to do some teaching on gender-related issues and God-centred sexuality. One particular privilege was being asked to speak to the following year's Leadership Academy students on the topic. My past disposition had now become a tool in God's hands to equip and empower emerging leaders and so serve God's people.

Finding solid, God-centred teaching about sex, gender and

sexuality is hard in most churches I have visited. In some it is non-existent. Maybe it's because it isn't the easiest topic in the world to approach. I mean, let's face it, the fear of offending others, or causing hurt, or just opening a can of worms without having enough knowledge, wisdom or resources to deal with what might tumble out, is just too daunting for many. So they avoid it altogether. But God knows what needs are present in people's hearts, minds and lives. And if we are honest, sexuality and gender are topics that interest, intrigue or fascinate many of us. So we must be bold and remember, God has the answers and he wants his people to be well-equipped and whole in these areas, so that they in turn can help others.

It can be extremely difficult to start a conversation about gender and sexuality, because they are very personal issues. So most people have their guards up when someone tries to approach them on these issues, for fear of being judged and rejected. Does that mean we should not go there? No. But if I can use an example, this subject is a honeybee not a panda! Think for a minute – pandas are soft and cuddly, so people are drawn to them and give generously to ensure they are protected and so on. Pandas get a high emotional response from people. But in reality, even if pandas did become extinct, life would still go on and most people's lives would be unaffected. Then consider the honeybee – not a good seller as a cuddly toy! Not very endearing and unlikely to be a candidate for conservation because they simply do not provoke the same emotional response from an audience. But if they became extinct, the world would be in a mess because they are essential for pollinating most crops, fruit and vegetables. In truth, the world cannot survive without the presence of the honeybee; it is we who would become extinct!

A similar thing to this happens in churches. If we show an

ill-treated, hungry child or an abused woman to the crowd, we all well up and respond out of compassion towards them. But if we present a man or woman suffering from gender dysphoria, someone in drag or in some form of sexual immorality, we get a different response all together. It is often one of judgement, revulsion, confusion and apathy. Or even worse, it becomes a laughing matter. These are the 'honeybees'; not cuddly, based on our stereotypical views, but every one of them essential in God's purpose; every one of them a person with pain in their soul that only Jesus can heal.

I hope you understand me. This topic of sexuality and gender is not 'warm and cuddly' and doesn't sell well, but I am going there through the vehicle of Gender Plus.

Have you ever wondered how God feels about it all? He is not drawn towards the 'warm and cuddly' over any other kind of person. No, in his sight all are equal and all can be healed, restored and forgiven. He sees right into the heart of each human being and knows the intricacy of their make-up. He loves all people just the same, and waits patiently for them to come as they are to him, with all their sin and shame, to be healed, restored and given 'life in all its fullness' (John 10:10, NCV).

That's why I have decided to give the rest of my life to help the 'honeybees' through the ministry of Gender Plus. The need is enormous, but God's love and grace are greater than it all.

Today, Samantha and I are getting on with our lives. She continues to work in the hospitals and I cut hair. We live in Bradford these days and are very involved in the community life of Life Church. But our passion is to reach people, especially people like the old me who are trapped in gender and sexual confusion.

Our prayer is that my story will inspire you to help the

'honeybees' too. To take up the challenge of equipping yourself to better understand what God says about the essential state of humanity, and to get to grips with the reality of sexual sin. People you know are struggling with these issues today. And they just need to know you love them, will accept them unconditionally, and help them find clarity about their true identity.

There is nothing to fear from a cross-dresser, gay or lesbian person; they may look different but they are just people with issues, just like you. Maybe yours were more 'cuddly' and someone reached out to you. But you needed them to. How much more do these 'honeybees' need you to reach out to them today?

Gender Plus can help by giving you information, education and tools to help those with gender and sexuality issues. We may be able to talk to you, train your team, or point you to others who can. If we can help, we will, for we are on a mission to bring freedom to the captives.

If you are trying to understand what the Bible teaches about homosexuality, marriage, or sexual immorality, you will find articles on our website to equip you to minister from a place of well-informed compassion. So please do have a browse through its pages at genderplus.co.uk

I encourage everyone to read biographies and articles that encourage healthy gender development, sexuality and sex. Listen to as much Bible-based teaching as you can, some of which you will find links to on our website.

There could be a tailor-made resource available, just for you.

Finally, let me say that no created being, charity, church or ministry on earth can heal or cure immorality, gender dysphoria or gayness. But when a sinner, a sexually broken, immoral or gay person meets Jesus, they have an opportunity to change.

It is only by the blood of Jesus that sins are forgiven, hearts are healed and people are freed-up from whatever mindset or bondage they are in.

Some say that there is no room for a person who calls himself a gay or homosexual in heaven. Well, as you have read, I used to call myself those things and I will be there! That's because God deals with sin, sin of any name or expression. Anyone who is caught up in any form of immorality, including homosexuality, has the same opportunity to become a 'new man or woman' and enter the kingdom of God through Jesus. He gives them a new name. No longer are they called gay, adulterer, pervert, porn star or immoral, but son, daughter and child of God, loved and fully accepted as a new person in Christ. The old has gone; the new has come (see 2 Corinthians 5:17).

I tell you my story fully convinced that I am just like those messed-up Corinthian Christians to whom Paul said:

Do not be deceived: neither the sexually immoral nor idolaters nor adulterers nor men who have sex with men nor thieves nor the greedy nor drunkards nor slanderers nor swindlers will inherit the kingdom of God. *And that is what some of you were.* But you were washed, you were sanctified, you were justified in the name of the Lord Jesus Christ and by the Spirit of our God.

(1 Corinthians 6:9–11, emphasis mine)

My closing prayer for all who read this book is that you enter into a relationship with Jesus. Just come as you are and give your life fully to him. No life is ever too far gone for God to rescue and make whole. He is patiently waiting for you, and his awesome life awaits your decision to choose him today.

Choose Jesus. Choose life. Then choose to help the 'honeybees'.

+ + +

If you would like to talk to someone about the issues raised in this book please contact:

gender +

Gender Plus – an organisation providing support and resources for those wanting to discover all that they are called to be in Christ, especially concerning God-centred gender and sexuality.

website: www.genderplus.co.uk
email: info@gender-plus.co.uk

If you would like to enquire about confidential counselling for any situation you may be facing, please contact:

grace4counselling@gmail.com